CULINARY
ATLANTA

Guide to the Best Restaurants, Markets, Food Tours, Breweries and More

Malika Bowling

ISBN-13: 978-1539918400
ISBN-10: 1539918408

About the Author

Malika Bowling has been writing about food for nearly a decade. She began it as a fun project, starting Atlanta Restaurant Blog (www.AtlantaRestaurantBlog.com). From there, she went on to author the Food Lovers' Guide to Atlanta and has been a contributing writing to USA Today as well as being featured on HGTV and The Huffington Post. She's also judged many food festivals and culinary competitions throughout Atlanta including Taste of Atlanta.

Malika believes that an exceptional meal can be found just as easily at a hole in the wall as in swanky establishments. When she's not checking off items on her travel bucket list or eating her way through Atlanta, she works as a digital consultant, creating brilliant content for company blogs, newsletters social media and videos. She lives in Atlanta with her husband, Glen (the amazing photographer behind most of the pictures on her blog and in this book).

FOREWORD
by Doc Lawrence

first met Malika Bowling several years ago at a media dinner in an Atlanta restaurant in Inman Park and was impressed by her observations and queries about the dishes served by the restaurant chef: Crisp, intelligent and to the point without a trace of self-promotion.

From that evening on, I have enjoyed and greatly benefited from Malika's brilliant restaurant reviews and commentary, even having the pleasure of dining with her at some of the ones in *Culinary Atlanta*, her masterfully composed and highly useful book. Integrity, independence, fairness and a keen eye for detail are hallmarks of her work as veteran restaurant critic.

Few reviewer/critics would dare to undertake the vastness of this effort, a monumental task when you take into account that she has not avoided the daunting task of discussing experiences at restaurants where many of us would be unfamiliar with the culinary culture. A case in point is her tour de force of the great places to dine in Atlanta's Buford Highway corridor.

Whether Korean, Vietnamese, Malaysian, Mexican or otherwise, Malika, guided by her very sophisticated palate and an open mind, shares impressions that merit reader trust.

My earliest restaurant experience was during childhood with visits to Atlanta landmarks like fabled Mary Mac's Tea Room and The Colonnade. The restaurant explosion, in my opinion, began shortly after the 1996 Atlanta Summer Olympics when the world got a taste of our Southern cuisine and became familiar with a growing diverse and sophisticated population. The table was set for the restaurant explosion through the efforts by gourmet pioneers like Jim Sanders. His restaurants, wine stores and wine classes educated thousands.

If Sanders was alive today, I believe he would join in praising the hard work displayed on the pages of *Culinary Atlanta* and recognize how useful it is for those who seek new tastes and flavors but are wary of going blind into unfamiliar restaurants.

Malika Bowling has dined at each place in her book, taking the time to sample dishes and examine not only the menu but the wine list and cocktail offerings as well. She knows the management, chefs and kitchen staff. For her, every meal is a new beginning. What you read from her is what you may reasonably expect from any of these restaurants.

Whether you live in the Atlanta region or visit our great part of America, *Culinary Atlanta* is your vital and highly useful guide for a better dining adventure. Read and learn. You'll understand why Malika Bowling is more than a fast rising star: Highly talented, she is destined for big things in the near future.

I hope we can keep her.

Atlanta native and veteran journalist Doc Lawrence co-authored "Southern Thymes Shared," with Emmy Award winning chef Lara Lyn Carter and is currently writing "Requiem for a Wine Taster," a screenplay based on one day in the life of Dr. Martin Luther King, Jr.

CONTENTS

Introduction

There are over 30 streets in Atlanta named Peachtree. To some we are known as the Peach State, although Georgia isn't number one in Peach production. If you've never been to Atlanta, you may think it is full of Southern food, like Shrimp 'N Grits and fried Okra. While these Southern favorites can be found, Atlanta has so much more to offer. Atlanta has become quite an eclectic mix of foods thanks to our diverse population, talented chefs and foodie community.

Atlanta is the hub of the Southeastern United States, with the world's busiest airport, the second largest convention center in the world and the home to many large corporations like Delta, Home Depot and Coca-Cola just to name a few. With the large number of visitors to Atlanta, it is paramount that there be a diverse cuisine available for these discerning tourists. However, the population of nearly 6 million, which includes the metro area, demands a variety of upscale dishes too.

Atlanta boasts many award-winning chefs and ones that have been featured on TV shows like Top Chef and a myriad of Food Network shows. Most have chosen to remain in Atlanta and continue to share their skills with us, whether that is taking the helm at a well-known and established restaurant or starting their own unique concept. Atlanta foodies and Bloggers are extremely supportive of these talented folks and spread the word about new ventures to keep others in the know.

We Atlantans love our burgers, pizza and barbecue. These are casual comfort foods that can be enjoyed by all and bring groups together. Even though we are full of these types of restaurants, we always welcome newcomers, whether they are traditional or have a unique spin on a tried and true concept. However, we still appreciate the finer foods, and the occasional offal, many of us not blinking an eye at the thought of eating Veal Sweetbreads or Bone Marrow.

When I moved to Atlanta in 1985, I remember stopping on the roadside to buy peaches and tomatoes from homeowners who grew them as a hobby. That all vanished as people began purchasing fruits and vegetables (whether seasonal or not) from large grocers. In recent years, Atlantans have realized the importance of eating fresh foods that haven't been treated with harmful pesticides or growth hormones. This has led to not only backyard home gardens and farmer's markets, but chefs have embraced the trend as well, buying fresh, organic produce from local markets or even adding gardens to their restaurants to grow their own herbs. It has been a pleasure to see the food cycle come full circle.

With the Atlanta Food and Wine Festival, chefs came from as far west as Texas and as far north as Virginia to participate in the festival. The inaugural festival solidified Atlanta to the rest of the country that Atlanta is truly a culinary destination and so much more than fried foods and moonshine.

The love of food has turned a passion into a career for some Atlanta residents, even pushing them into a new career that they may not have intended. Not many would disagree in the last handful of years our economy changed forever. Even extremely educated people were forced out of their jobs. This has spawned careers some never knew they had in them and helped shape the food scene of Atlanta. Some of these include food trucks, catering and secret suppers and underground food events some of which would not exist had it been for those fearless individuals that took on a new career.

So, who is this book for? Really anyone who has an interest in food and wants to further explore what Atlanta has to offer. Whether you are in Atlanta for a couple days, a new transplant unsure of where to start your food exploration or someone who's lived in the city for a while, this book can serve as a guide. If you've only got a couple days in Atlanta but want to make sure you explore destinations off the beaten path, the guide book will help. And if you've lived in Atlanta for years, and have always wanted to explore the ethnic mecca that is Buford Highway, there are lots of restaurants listed that can serve as a guide for you too. My hope is that you will explore places outside your comfort zone whether that be ubering to an unfamiliar neighborhood in search of a fabulous dining experience or the taste of a new cuisine you haven't yet had the tenacity to try.

CHAPTER 1
Festivals and Markets

FOOD FESTIVALS

Atlanta is a very active city, blessed with warm weather from early spring to late fall, allowing for many outdoor festivals. Many of these festivals center around food. They are listed below according to when they occur.

FEBRUARY

Oysterfest

Oysterfest is a 2-day event that takes place in Atlanta, although the venue has changed from year to year. Besides sampling different types of oysters, attendees can sample beer hear live music. Tickets should be purchased in advance and are not inclusive of food or drinks. Geared to adults, kiddies should be left at home.

MARCH

Baconfest www.baconfestatl.com

This pork-lover event takes place in late March. It takes place in the parking lot of Dad's Garage Theater, an improvisational comedy theater. Entertainment includes live music, improv games, and eating contests. Various price levels starting at $25 for a taste sampling and all the way up to all you can eat and drink. The festival takes place rain or shine. No kids or dogs allowed. This event sells out each year, so purchasing tickets in advance is strongly recommended.

APRIL

Dogwood Festival www.dogwood.org

The first of many spring festivals in Atlanta, the Dogwood Festival is one of the most anticipated. Many look forward to it as it has many activities that appeal to a wide audience. Activities include artwork from more than 200 artists, live music, and an activity zone for kids. Foodies will enjoy plenty of food trucks. Some homeowners also open up their beautiful homes as part of the festival. Fun for the entire family.

Inman Park Festival www.inmanparkfestival.org

The Inman Park Festival and Tour of Homes takes place the last weekend in April. At Inman Park, Euclid Avenue at Elizabeth Street, in Atlanta, the festival not only has lots of arts and crafts, a street market and live entertainment, but even a parade. The parade takes place Saturday afternoon and is headed up by the Inman Park Butterfly. They'll be lots of good food on hand and even a tour of homes. Note that while the festival itself is free, touring the homes requires a ticket purchase of around $15.

Sweetwater 420 Festival www.sweetwater420fest.com

This is a 3-day festival, celebrating Earth Day. It takes place at Centennial Olympic Park in downtown Atlanta. Besides beer, food and live music, there is an artist's market that includes clothes, jewelry, accessories and other goodies. Admission starts at >$40 per ticket for a one-day pass and guests must have a wristband as proof of ticket purchase.

MAY

Food That Rocks www.foodthatrocks.org

Held on a Saturday evening, Food that Rocks features around 25 restaurants from the Sandy Springs area. And as the name suggests, music is a big part of the festival that takes place in Hammond Park. Unlike other "Taste of" events admission is NOT free. Cost is $55 in advance and $65 at the door and is all inclusive of tastes.

Marietta Greek Festival www.mariettagreekfestival.org

Lesser known than the Atlanta Greek Festival, the Marietta Greek Festival, taking place four months earlier, attracts quite a crowd as well. The festival includes authentic Greek food like Souvlaki, Gyros and of course Baklava for dessert. Throughout the day there is live entertainment of music and dancing. Dancers vary in age from quite young at the kinder-garten level to young adults and are outfitted in Greek cloth-ing. There is actually a Greek colosseum on church grounds that allow great views of the dancers. This in itself is a pretty spectacular sight. Don't miss the Church tour. In less than

30 minutes you'll get to see the beautiful architecture and design and a small group. Admission is only $2.

Smoke on the Lake Festival www.smokeonthelake.org

Taking place over two days during early May, this barbecue festival features live music on the water in the northern suburbs of Atlanta, at Lake Acworth. Admission is free but if you want to stay for several hours listening to the variety of musical acts and sampling barbecue, you should buy a table, which come with six chairs for $100. You'll pay for samples and proceeds benefit various charities.

Taste of Marietta www.tasteofmarietta.com

Taste of Marietta has been increasingly drawing a bigger crowd each year to their festival that occurs in late spring. Held on one day only, Sunday, over 70 restaurants participate in the festival. The festival includes live music all day long, multiple moonwalks and games, sand art, face painting and more! For the kids, there is lots of entertainment as well. Admission is free but tastes range from $1 to $4. Free parking is available in many of the nearby Cobb Government building parking decks.

Taste of Alpharetta www.awesomealpharetta.com/what-to-do/taste-of-alpharetta

Although somewhat unusual, the Taste of Alpharetta takes place on a Thursday evening – one day only. Taste of Alpharetta is in Downtown Alpharetta at Wills Park. Over 50 restaurants participate. Sample appetizers, entrees and desserts from the top restaurants in Alpharetta. The Taste of Alpharetta also includes culinary demonstrations, activities and entertainment. Admission is free, but food samples are priced at $1-3 per food sample. Parking can be difficult, so arrive as early as possible to ensure good parking.

Taste of the Nation www.atlantataste.org

Taste of the Nation takes place at the Georgia Aquarium. Over the course of an evening, guests enjoy tastes from top Atlanta restaurants all for a good cause – to help end childhood hunger. Taste of the Nation has been in Atlanta for over a decade. More than 50 of Atlanta's top restaurants participate offering up tasty dishes and wonderful wines. General admission is $250 for gala that goes from 7:30 - 10:00 p.m. VIP ticket purchasers ($350 per person) enter at 6:30 p.m. for the preview party.

JUNE

Atlanta Food and Wine Festival www.atlfoodandwinefestival.com

Inspired by the Food and Wine Classic in Aspen, this is the most exciting festival for Atlanta as far as foodies are concerned. Drawing festival-goers from not only different states but different countries, it is a celebration of the new south and the popularity of its food and talent of its chefs. Guests get to sip, taste and learn about Southern food through a series of well-planned seminars, demonstrations and tasting experiences. The Food and Wine festival will represent the best restaurants and chefs from Texas to D.C. and the states in between. Tickets for the Atlanta Food & Wine Festival range from $75 for select tastings tents to the $2500 Connoisseur Package, which includes access to the exclusive tastings, seminars and demonstrations.

Virginia Highland Summer Fest www.vahi.org/summer-fest.html

The Virginia Highlands Summerfest takes place along Virginia Avenue in the heart of the Virginia Highlands neighborhood. Summerfest includes arts, foods and live music and is a great event for the whole family. For the children, there is Kidsfest with lots of activities. Admission is free.

AUGUST

Grant Park Summer Shade Festival www.summershadefestival.org

The festival encourages people to enjoy the century old trees in historic Grant Park. There is a 5k run on Saturday morning and an Artist Market as well as Live entertainment. For kids there is a fun center. Atlanta's top chefs will offer special samples. Taste some great wines and ales that are offered at Atlanta's top restaurants. Regular admission is free. VIP Tickets are $75.

Pigs N Peaches BBQ Festival www.PigsAndPeaches.com

Taking place in Kennesaw, the Pigs N Peaches BBQ Festival is a two-day festival that has garnered a tremendous following. There is BBQ for sale from different vendors, a BBQ Cook Off, and even a Farmer's Market. There is also free music from a number of local and national acts, a large Kid Zone, and other exhibits with unique products for sale. Admission is free and parking is free in nearby lots.

SEPTEMBER

Atlanta Greek Festival www.atlantagreekfestival.org

Taking place in late September, the Atlanta Greek Festival is a weekend long celebration that draws in people from all over the Greater Atlanta area. Entertainment includes Greek dancing and traditional Greek food. Inside the Greek Church, artists sell their goods including jewelry. Tours of the church are available as well. Entry is $5. Buy tickets in advance online for additional savings in multiple quantities.

OCTOBER

Taste of Atlanta www.tasteofatlanta.com

An all-encompassing food festival, the Taste of Atlanta, draws food lovers from all over the Southeast. The festival taking placed from Friday to Sunday in the latter part of the month, showcases the diverse food and restaurants in Atlanta. Foodies gather to sample an enormous amount of tastes from more than 70 restaurants, live entertainment and special cooking demos. Regular admission is $25 per day and includes a wristband preloaded with taste points to redeem samples. In addition to regular admission, there's also a special VIP area of tasting tents and beer and wine tent. VIP Packages are $75 per day.

MARKETS

Buford Highway Farmer's Market 5600 Buford Highway, Atlanta, GA 30340; (770) 455-0770 www.aofwc.com

When you hear the words "Buford Highway" you think of a pop up open-air type setting, but that's not what this gigantic market is. The mammoth spot (it's about 100,000 square feet) is a huge grocery store carrying a wide variety of ethnic foods. Need dried Persimmon, Indian Bitter Melon, Thai Okra? You'll find these and plenty more hard to find fruits and vegetables. But that's just one section of the grocery. You'll find plenty of snacks to tickle your palate like Cuttlefish flavored crackers or spicy flavored sticks to give your cerveza a kick.

One of the most interesting areas is the seafood department, with just about every edible creature from the sea found here. Choose from eight different ways to have your fish cut. Tip: Go on weekdays to avoid the frantic crowds that shop on weekends. Plus they have a cafeteria you can enjoy lunch before or after you shop.

Krog Street Market 99 Krog Street, Atlanta, Ga 30307; (770) 434-2400 www.krogstreetmarket.com

Though it sat empty for years, the factory building was converted into a modern food market. This Inman Park hot spot was modeled after the famous food stalls in New York and Seattle. Pull up a stool at Hop City and enjoy a glass of wine or beer while people watching. Here you can see many of the food stalls and decide which cuisine you have an appetite for.

This takes food court dining to a new level. Here, you'll find Gu's Dumplings, a spin-off from a popular Buford Highway restaurant, Yalla with its Mediterranean fare, along with G.C. Barbecue offering up some delectable 'cue. Just want a sandwich? You can get that at Fred's Meat and Bread.

Looking for a sit-down restaurant? The options are diverse. Top Chef contestant, Eli Kirshtein serves his interpretation of French cuisine at The Luminary. The high-energy spot, Craft Izakaya, serves expert cocktails and killer menu of sushi and tapas, perfect for a group outing. Well-known chef Ford Fry has a Tex-Mex spot, Superica here as well. The restored factory is adjacent to the Atlanta Beltline for a stroll after you've filled your belly. Heads up, you might even spot a celebrity while dining here.

Ponce City Market 675 Ponce de Leon Ave, Atlanta, GA 30308; (404) 900-7900 www.poncecitymarket.com

Ponce City Market is the latest in refurbished historical buildings. Plus it is where to find the hottest chefs in the southeast, or at least their restaurants. Here's where to find food stalls by Linton Hopkins, Anne Quatrano and Sean Brock, plus many more local, well-known chefs. The heart of what was once the Sears, Roebuck and Co. building is the central food hall with many food purveyors. Besides restaurants, here you'll find Tap on Ponce that features both beer and wine on tap, Saint Germain with a selection of artisan pastries as well as 18.21 Bitters offering premium cocktail mixers.

Fall and spring are the prefect times to visit the city's rooftop gaming spot, Skyline Park. With stunning views of Atlanta and boardwalk style games like putt putt golf and skee ball, it is the perfect spot to take out of town guests. Besides the games, there's also a beer garden and carnival style foods that are reasonably priced.

Ponce City Market is also a mecca of international cuisine from Biltong Bar featuring South African favorites, India with Botiwalla, the Moroccan flavors of Marrakesh all the way to Szechuan restaurant, Jia. Plus, don't miss Top Chef Contestant, Hector Santiago's El Super Pan. The Latin influenced cuisine includes sandwiches like the Cuban and Media Noche with portions large enough to make multiple meals.

Sweet Auburn Market 209 Edgewood Ave, Atlanta, GA 30303; (404) 659- 1665 www.thecurbmarket.com

Need pig ears, frog legs, or oxtail? Open since 1924, the Sweet Auburn Curb Market located downtown, offers a variety of fresh fruits and vegetables, meats and seafood. In addition, there are several small cafes to stop for a bite before or after shopping. Stop by Grindhouse Killer Burger for delicious burgers to fuel up before or after shopping. A favorite for sweets is Miss D's New Orleans Pralines. Arriving in Atlanta after Katrina struck New Orleans, Miss D started selling her goods here. Besides pralines, made with Georgia pecans, you'll find flavored popcorn varieties.

For a taste of true southern food visit Metro Deli Soul Food. With favorites like collard greens, mac n cheese, sweet potato casserole, and meatloaf, this is certainly the place to get your fill of southern fixings. Swing by the Sweet Auburn Bakery for their Sweet Potato Cheesecake. You'll have to pay to park there, or you can take the Atlanta Streetcar Trolley from the downtown Peachtree Center MARTA station.

CHAPTER 2
Buckhead

For many years, Buckhead sparkled by day as the swanky spot for shopping, working and socializing. At night, it drew in the younger crowd with a myriad of bars that young professionals flocked to. While there are still many skyscrapers and posh boutiques, the post –college nightlife scene has been transformed to more upscale restaurants, shopping and condos.

The "Buckhead Betties" or "ladies who lunch," a many refer to them, are still found around town at the upscale eateries. Many conventioneers prefer to stay in Buckhead versus Downtown for the numerous restaurants that are easily accessible and within walking distance of hotels. As Buckhead continues to evolve, one thing remains constant: It will long be the epitome of Atlanta with its modern look and feel mixed with its distinct Southern charm.

1Kept 2293 Peachtree Rd., Atlanta, GA 30309; (404) 254-1973
www.1kept.com

1 Kept is a not-so-secret gastropub located in Peachtree
Hills. With its low lighting and rich woods, it's a super spot
to meet for a drink before dinner elsewhere. There are also a
couple comfy chairs near the bar area that offer a bit more
privacy. Whether you are looking for beer, wine or cocktails,
there's something for you. There are about a dozen wines
by the glass and nearly 20 craft beer choices. Try the 50 /50
martini, half vodka, half gin (hence the name 50 /50) made
with fresh basil, cilantro and ginger beer. Scallops, Flatbreads
and Schnitzel with Gnocchi are all winning dishes. $$

Cinebistro www.cinebristro.com/brookhaven

This is the best movie / dining experience you can find in Atlanta. The interior lobby is so gorgeous you may just want to hang there and have a cocktail. Theatres feature stadium seating and comfy chairs. Food quality is on par or even slightly better than area restaurants and worth the price. You can order tickets online and select you seats. No kids are allowed in the evenings. $$$

10 Degrees South 4183 Roswell Rd., Atlanta, GA 30342; (404) 705-8870   www.10degreessouth.com

Opened in 1998, 10 Degrees South is one of those charming, classy restaurants that for whatever reason, stays under the radar in the Atlanta dining scene. Once the only South African restaurant in Atlanta, the owner has since expanded his offerings with other restaurants around Atlanta. The calamari is a must as are the Sosaties, a skewered beef in an apricot curry sauce. For something authentically South African, order the Bobotie, a sweet ground beef mixture topped with custard. Think of it as South African Shepherd's Pie. Instead of peas, carrots etc., this "pie" of sorts has apples, apricots and raisins. As a side dish, the Sambals are the South African version of grits. While there are items for non-adventurous eaters on the menu, it is worth exploring the unique menu offerings, as they are all standouts. $$$

Anis 2974 Grandview Ave., Atlanta, GA 30305; (404) 233-9889 www.anisbistro.com

Known for its lovely patio, Anis blends chic and sophistication at the same time. You'll feel as if you were invited into a good friend's house for a meal, rather than at some stuffy restaurant. As this is French, don't miss out on the Moules

Marinieres – mussels in garlicky, buttery sauce. Steaks are a hit, but fish doesn't disappoint. On weekends they have live music. It is worth mentioning again that the patio is lovely. Opt for sitting here whenever possible. $$

Aria 490 E. Paces Ferry Rd., Atlanta, GA 30305; (404) 233-7673 www.aria-atl.com

An elegant and classy establishment, Aria has been a Buckhead fixture for years. The white linens and walls a stark contrast with the dark floor and ceiling, but they add up to a beautiful surrounding with a one of a kind ornate lighting fixture that hangs above the main dining room. This is more of a romantic place for couples or double dates (think anniversary celebrations). Start with the Foie Gras with vanilla glazed fuji apple and arugula or the Lobster Cocktail. The beef short rib is one of the most flavorful and tender you'll find anywhere. The lamb Chef and owner Gerry Kalaska is extremely focused on the farm to table movement, which is evident in the menu. $$$$

Atlanta Fish Market 265 Pharr Rd, Atlanta, GA 30305; (404) 262-3165 www.buckheadrestaurants.com

Part of the Buckhead Life Restaurant Group, you can't miss this restaurant, as it is the one that has the big fish atop the roof. Upon entering, your eyes will feast on the beautiful display of fish in the ice case. Sushi is prevalent on the menu, although it isn't a sushi restaurant. This is the kind of restaurant that presents the classics – Clam Chowder, Stuffed Flounder, Lobster tails, etc. The options aren't new or trendy, but more tried and true. There are many seafood options and lots of fresh fish can be found. Reservations are a must, even if it is a weeknight. $$$

Basil's 2985 Grandview Ave., Atlanta, GA 30305; (404) 233-9755 www.Basils.net

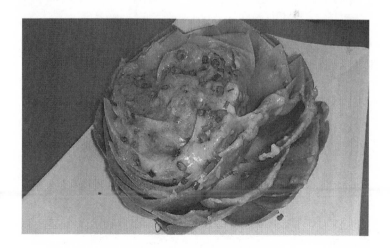

Basil's has been a long time favorite of Buckhead residents. One—for their gorgeous patio and two—for their incredible Mediterranean influenced dishes. They make a mean cocktail, too. Ask for the Andes Candies Cocktail. Get the Artichoke appetizer or Flatbread. The Lamb Chops are phenomenal, as are steaks here. $$$

Bhojanic 3400 Around Lenox Road, Ste 201 Atlanta, GA 30326; (404) 841 -8472 www.bhojanic.com

Although the décor is somewhat minimalist, it works well for the space. Portions are pretty large, especially for the Thali, which is quite possible to make two meals out of. Don't miss out their Mango Lassi, Vegetable Samosa or Goat Curry. You'll want to place several orders for the Garlic Naan as it comes hot and fresh and disappears rather quickly. For those who enjoy hot and spicy, order the Chicken 65. It is also family friendly. Tip: The Lunch Express deal features a samosa, side salad, choice of meat and vegetables. $$

Bistro Niko 3344 Peachtree Rd., Atlanta, GA 30319; (404) 261-6456 www.buckheadrestaurants.com

This French restaurant is another restaurant part of the famed Buckhead Life Restaurant Group. It is truly a beautiful dining space. Entering the restaurant, you'll pass by the open kitchen, which showcases their meats in a glass display. The colorful and well-appointed décor makes for an enjoyable lunch or dinner and you'll find the place buzzing during both occasions, not slowing down at all. Start with the stuffed Piquillo Peppers stuffed with cod and potatoes, the Ravioli or the Smoked Salmon Sandwiches. If you are trying to eat light, any of these are good options for a small meal. Duck is always a solid menu choice. While the menu lends itself to romantic dining, bear in mind that the dining area is large and quite loud. So, if a quiet, intimate evening is what you are seeking, you probably won't find it here. Reservations are a must. $$$

Blue Ridge Grill 1261 W. Paces Ferry Rd, Atlanta, GA 30327; (404) 233-5030 www.blueridgegrill.com

An Atlanta classic, the interior resembles an upscale log cabin, with the name paying homage to the Blue Ridge Mountains in North Georgia. Some of the signature items are the Georgia Trout and Horseradish Crusted Grouper. Meat lovers will enjoy the 20-ounce Ribeye. Oenophiles will love the extensive wine list, presented on an iPad. The dinner and lunch menus are almost identical, so if you are looking to spend less, visit at lunch and you won't miss anything. The downstairs features a private dining area that can fit up to 45 people. $$$

Bone's 3130 Piedmont Rd., Atlanta, GA 30305; (404) 237-2663 www.bonesrestaurant.com

This well-established steak house has been an Atlanta institution for over 30 years. As the name may suggest, this is a steak house, and a high-end one at that. Don't expect trendy here, but do expect exceptional service and steaks. Great for groups and the seafood platter with crab, jumbo shrimp and lobster is perfect with a group to share. Beef Carpaccio is a notable starter. The New York Strip is probably the most popular and best steak on the menu. $$$$

Bucket Shop 3475 Lenox Rd. #220, Atlanta, GA 30326; (404) 261-9244 www.bucketshopcafe.com

This Buckhead bar has been around for quite some time and is extremely popular for its patio. The food is primarily bar food—wings, mozzarella sticks, and burgers. Out-of-towners will appreciate that you can get bar food here late at night. Arriving on a flight late and looking for something other than hotel food? Head to this prime Buckhead spot for decent bar food. A good spot for college football viewing! Menu highlights: Burgers, Jack Daniels Wings. $$

Buckhead Diner 3073 Piedmont Rd., Atlanta, GA 30305; (404) 262 3336   www.buckheadrestaurants.com/buckhead-diner

The neon glow and shiny chrome exterior scream Diner, but put aside any notions you have of a typical diner, as this isn't your average diner. Maytag Blue Cheese Chips are one of the best starters on the menu. Fish lovers shouldn't miss out on the Mahi Mahi tostada. Don't forget to save room for dessert. The Key Lime pie and Banana Crème pie (James Beard award-winning), while not the most inventive, are still fabulous. Trivia: When Giada de Laurentis visited, she declared that she loved their banana crème pie. Note that they don't take reservations. $$$

C&S Oyster Bar   3240 Cobb Parkway, Atlanta, GA 30339; (770) 272-0999   www.candsoysterbar.com

Surprisingly, this fancy spot has thrived, while being located in a strip mall its entire existence. Once inside you'll feel like you've been transported to a 1920's speakeasy. It's a great place to go if you are on the company expense account. The white-gloved servers hand you hot towels before you begin your seafood binge. Start with a classic cocktail before moving on to wine. Make sure to take advantage of the daily oyster specials. Fresh fish and seafood are flown in daily. Skip the pricey lobster tails and Crab Legs in favor of fresh fish. Snapper, Tuna, Skate, Sea Bass, Flounder all are exceptional and are available in choice of preparation and sauce. $$$$

Café Agora 262 E. Paces Ferry Rd., Atlanta, GA 30305; (404) 949-0900   www.cafeagora.com

This Turkish / Mediterranean restaurant is located in the middle of all the Buckhead action. Café Agora has been around for quite a while and garnered a pretty loyal follow-ing. The restaurant has only about eight to ten tables. Most patrons get their food to go. However, it is a great spot if you are dining alone. The Mezze plate is the perfect start, allow-ing for a sampling of the most popular items. This includes Dolmas (stuffed grape leaves), Hummus, Baba Ganoush, Tabouleh, and Hvuc Ezme (a carrot salad). If your party is small this will be rather filling, but the Gyro is not to be missed. $$

Canoe   4199 Paces Ferry Rd., Atlanta, GA 30339; (770) 432-2663 www.canoeatl.com[1]

This is a beautiful setting just on the cusp of Buckhead. Popular for a special occasion, the décor is lush and beautiful. Service is top notch and perfect to bring out of town guests. The cuisine is upscale but not too fussy. Start your meal with the BBQ Shrimp or Salt and Pepper Calamari. If you are feeling adventurous, get the Kangaroo. One of the highlights here is their weekend Brunch. The variety is outstanding and the view of the outside patio, manicured lawn and river just add even more to the ambience. Tip: Make sure you visit during daylight, to see the beautiful river view. Reservations Recommended. $$$$

Chops   70 W. Paces Ferry Rd., Atlanta, GA 30305; (404) 262-2675 www.buckheadrestaurants.com

Another restaurant that is part of the Buckhead Life Restaurant Group, Chops is very high and very pricey. Waiters wear jackets and service here is impeccable. Many business outings are held here and the noise level can get rather high. For a romantic date, a weekend evening would be a better time to visit. Start with the fried Lobster tail served up with some honey mustard. This is perfection. For mains, order the Filet, NY Strip or the Ribeye, but skip the Wagyu steak. Side sauces such as béarnaise sauce are optional, but the steaks are done perfectly and the addition of any sauce is unnecessary. Reservations are a must. $$$$

Chow Bing 3330 Piedmont Rd. NE #22B, Atlanta, GA 30305; (404) 816-8008 www.chowbing.com

Gary Lin, founder and owner of Chow Bing, wants to show guests that healthy Chinese food—made largely with organic food—does exist. That's what guests will find at Chow Bing. Get the Crispy Wontons or Bing Bowl (you choose your own ingredients like chicken, beef, rice, veggies, etc.) Options are quite affordable. $

Colonnade 1879 Cheshire Bridge Rd., Atlanta, GA 30324; (404) 874-5642   www.colonnadeatl.com

The Colonnade is a historic restaurant that has been around since the 1920s featuring traditional Southern food. This is where you visit or take out of town guests to sample Southern food. The décor is sorely in need of updating, but that is part of the charm of the restaurant. And if you are under the age of 65 you will probably be the young-est patron. Don't miss out on their fried chicken, fried pork chops, chicken livers, grits or sweet tea. And get the Coconut Crème pie. Colonnade has an Early Bird Special for $13, which includes entree, 2 sides, beverage, and dessert. It's available Mon.-Thur. 5-6:30pm, and Sat. 12-4pm. Note that they only take CASH. No credit cards accepted. $$

Cook Hall   3377 Peachtree Rd., Atlanta, GA 30326; (404) 523-3600   www.cookhallatlanta.com

Located at the Westin in Buckhead, Cook Hall treats guests to craft cocktails and a new American menu that impress-es. Think items like Poached Egg with Caviar and Crème Fraiche, Shaved Tuna with Chili Tapioca and Octopus in Black Pepper Sauce. Expect a lively atmosphere most nights, not the place for a quiet dinner. Tip: They have a lovely patio with fire pit for cool fall evenings. $$$

Dantanna's 3400 Around Lenox Rd., Atlanta, GA 30326; (404) 760-8873   www.dantannas.com

Dantanna's is a prime choice for after work or happy hour gatherings with your coworkers or pals. There are lots of TVs for sports watching. While the steak varieties are plenty, the Wasabi Tuna topped with lump crab, as well as the Cioppino (lobster, crab, shrimp, mussels and clams in a tomato broth) will make seafood lovers happy. There are also fifty wines available by the glass. Tip: While most people visit after work or for dinner, Dantanna's also serves up a pretty solid brunch. Options include: Fried Oysters Benedict , Shirred Eggs in Tulips (Two eggs baked in crepes with Maine lobster, shrimp and crawfish. $$$

Davio's   3500 Peachtree Rd, Atlanta, GA 30326; (404) 844-4810 www.davios.com/atl

Located in ritzy Phipps Plaza, Davio's Northern Italian Steakhouse is fancy, yet approachable. The large patio is often the site of mixers and work functions. The inside of the restaurant is much more impressive. The restaurant is known for their signature eggrolls with flavors like Philly Cheesesteak, Chicken Parm and others. Make sure to order the Gnocchi and steak. They always do excellent pastries, so make sure to save room for dessert. $$$$

Del Frisco's 3376 Peachtree Rd., Atlanta, GA 30326; (404) 537-2828 www.delfriscosgrille.com/atlanta

The Ahi tuna tacos are a signature item with a generous portion of tuna and can easily work as an entree. The crab cake, while amazing, is smaller, a tasty, yet not overly filling, starter. You'll certainly want to make sure to not fill up on appetizers, as steak is the star of the show here. You can't go wrong with the Ribeye. Some evenings, Del Frisco's has a special of three filets prepared with toppings of béarnaise, oscar and pork foie gras butter. $$$

Divan 3125 Piedmont Road, Atlanta, GA 30305; (404) 467-4297 www.divanatlanta.com

With a mix of Mediterranean and Persian, there's something to please everyone at this Buckhead hot spot. The Turkey Kufta with pomegranate glaze. A blackened salmon comes with a side of linguine Alfredo hitting the Mediterranean angle and bit the spicy lamb kabobs are all Persian. They have beautiful rooms for private parties too. For those who like to stay for the after-party, take advantage of their Hookah. $$$

Doraku The Shops Buckhead Atlanta, 267 East Paces Ferry Rd., Atlanta, GA 30305; (404) 842-0005 www.dorakusushi.com

Located in the Shops at Buckhead Atlanta, this Japanese restaurant offers many diverse dishes besides sushi. A Roasted Truffle Salmon is complex and blended with flavors you wouldn't expect. There's a guacamole sauce plus a Yuzu sauce. A Chicken Fried Octopus delights as well, and Executive Chef Todd Kulper insists on using fresh, never frozen octopus at all times. Ramen lovers should get the Sea Urchin pasta, perfect on a cold evening. Nigiri options include tuna, salmon, and grilled-in-butter King crab. Doraku sources their foods from all over; the tuna from Hawaii and the salmon from Faroe Island. Tip: There are specials every night of the week! $$$

Flip Burger Boutique - 3655 Roswell Rd., Atlanta, GA 30305; (404) 549-3298   www.flipburgerboutique.com

What's unique about yet another Burger Joint? Flip Burger is the brainchild of Top Chef Alumni, Richard Blais. The over-the-top décor with white leather seating, ornate mirrors and décor are matched by the burgers. Think lobster topped burgers, Ahi Tuna and Chorizo burgers with fried egg and paprika. Milkshakes are a fussy affair too. Gingerita shake made with Tequila, Ginger ice cream and lime sherbet. There is another location on the Westside. $$

Gypsy Kitchen 3035 Peachtree Rd., Atlanta, GA 30305; (404) 939-9840 www.gk-atl.com

The Shoppes at Buckhead Atlanta have a lovely spot in Gypsy Kitchen. The giant bull that hovers over the bar is a focal point. They make terrific cocktails and always have a decent happy hour. Their décor is so attractive guests may be willing to overlook the fact that the food can be hit or miss. Perfect for large groups, it is great for a birthday gathering. $$$

Hal's Kitchen Take a Cooking Class www.halskitchen.com

With a state of art kitchen featuring the latest appliances, you'll fall in love with this this spot and its instructors. Classes are fun and menus are interesting yet informative. It makes for a fun date or a fantastic team building activity for a work group. $$$$

Haven 1441 Dresden Dr., Atlanta, GA 30319; (404) 969-0700 www.havenrestaurant.com

Located very close to the hustle and bustle of Buckhead in the Brookhaven neighborhood, Haven is a restaurant adored by those that live in the area. Start with the Sweetbreads with Grits and the Mussels. Note that the menu does change seasonally. For entrees, steaks are highlights with a KC Strip and Ribeye being particularly wonderful. However, Georgia Trout and Scallops are quite nice, too. The patio is gorgeous and should absolutely be taken advantage of on warm days. The interior is pretty as well, but can get very loud when crowded. $$$

HOBNOB 1551 Piedmont Ave. Atlanta, GA 30324; (404) 968-2288   www.hobnobatlanta.com

Hobnob is similar to a pub with a fun patio. This seems the type of place where a group of friends might meet for drinks. Although they are open late, it is much more of a dinner crowd. Start with the Southern Spring Rolls stuffed with pork and collard greens. Get the Southerner burger with a fried green tomato, goat cheese, and a balsamic reduction. They have pizzas as well, and they are available with a gluten free crust. $$

Hoki Japanese Restaurant 3300 Cobb Parkway, Atlanta, GA 30339; (770) 690-0555 www.sushirestaurantinatlanta.com

Whether you want to have excellent sushi, or noodle bowls, you can't go wrong at Hoki Sushi in Vinings. For specialty rolls, get the Angel Fish or Tropical. It's a super choice for a date night, but as the space is small, not the best for a large group. If you want to experience the best, get the Omakase and let the chefs present the best appetizers, sushi and sashimi. Fancy dessert? Get the green tea Tiramisu. $$$

Holeman & Finch 2277 Peachtree Rd, Atlanta, GA 30309; (404) 948-1175   www.holeman-finch.com

This not-so-secret gastropub launched a couple years ago and it has been wowing visitors with its coveted burger ever since. There are no signs from the street, or even on the door for that matter, that the name is actually Holeman & Finch. You just have to know where it is. Hint: If you can find Restaurant Eugene then you can find H&F. The space is rather small, but gets crowded every night. The one commu-nal table in the middle of the restaurant seats most patrons. Ask your server to pick out a concoction for you and you won't be disappointed. Other menu items are the charcuterie plate, and offal like fried pig's ears and veal sweetbreads. If you are traveling by yourself this is a fun place to go, as it is rather easy to chat up other patrons. $$$

Industry Tavern 3280 Peachtree Road Northeast #187, Atlanta, GA 30305; (404) 254-4468 www.industrytavern. com

Though it is a sports bar, Industry Tavern serves elevated pub food. Think house made gnocchi and lobster risotto. Though the menus for lunch and dinner have quite a bit of overlap, heartier specials like a Lobster Nachos and NY Strip are only available at dinner. Slammed doesn't even begin to describe how busy this spot becomes at the noon hour. Your best bet is to visit for an early or late lunch or wait until the evening. A Thai Chicken Salad made with kale has a delicious peanut dressing. Try the Victory pie, which won as best in a Las Vegas pizza competition several years ago. A pesto and fennel sausage pizza was equally as delicious. Tip: No need to valet, as the restaurant will validate your parking for two hours in the Terminus lot. Happy hour lasts from 4:30 to 8 Mondays through Thursdays. $$

Kaleidescope 1410 Dresden Dr. Ste 100, Atlanta, GA 30319; (404) 474-9600   www.k-pub.com

A neighborhood pub slightly north of Buckhead in the Brookhaven community, Kaleidescope draws a crowd that are neighborhood residents, but also foodies that venture out for tasty and out of the ordinary items. The menu is diverse in that it includes inexpensive starters, small plates a tad more and full-blown entrees for those that want to indulge in a myriad of flavors. Start things off with the pork pot stickers. Their burger has won best burger in several burger competitions. It is piled with pimento cheese and chow chow is a stand out as is Shrimp n Grits. Beer lovers will appreciate the selection of craft beers. On the weekends be prepared to wait for a table, as they do not take reservations. However, they do take call-ahead seating. $$

King and Duke 3060 Peachtree St., Atlanta, GA 30305; (404) 477-3500   www.kinganddukeatl.com

The patio is lovely for spring or fall evenings. Upstairs is more seating that can be rented out for private events. Pimento Cheese Hushpuppies are sinfully gooey and stuffed with bits of ham. The wings, though only two per order are a fun twist on regular Buffalo wings. They come with a goat cheese sauce. Order the Pork Chop, nice and smoky and topped with seasonal fruit. Tip: Want to see the action up close?

They offer a chef's tasting menu Sunday to Thursdays from 6:00 to 8:45 pm. $$$

Kyma 3085 Piedmont Rd., Atlanta, GA 30305; (404) 262-0702 www.buckheadrestaurants.com

Yet another one of the Buckhead Life Restaurant Group, Kyma serves up contemporary Greek food in an upscale atmosphere. The décor is nothing short of stunning. Enter and see constellation display on the deep blue ceiling and the Greek white marble columns reminiscent of Greek architecture. If you are looking for some of the freshest seafood with Greek seasoning, than Kyma is the spot to go. The Octopus and Dolmades (stuffed grape leaves) are great starters. Fish is the standout here. The selection isn't huge, as they focus on a selection of top notch varieties. The Sole and Baramundi are two of the best choices to be had. Don't miss out on the loukoumades (deep fried doughnut balls that are soaked in a honey syrup) for dessert. Surprisingly, there is a wonderful kids menu. $$$$

Local Three 3290 Northside Pkwy. Ste. 120, Atlanta, GA 30327; (404) 968-2700 www.localthree.com

Local Three is a warm and welcoming pub-style restaurant. The servers are both friendly and knowledgeable about the upscale Southern menu. The farm to table food is sophisticated without having any pretentiousness to it. For starters, expect items like roasted Goat Empanada or Rabbit Tikka Masala. The Charcuterie plate, aptly named "Notorious P.I.G.", is lovely for sharing with dining companions. Note: the menu changes as to what is in season. Park in the garage next door and bring your receipt in to be validated. Reservations strongly encouraged. $$$

Nakato Japanese Restaurant - 1776 Cheshire Bridge Rd., Atlanta, GA 30324;

(404) 873-6582 www.nakatorestaurant.com

If you want to enjoy Japanese Hibachi in a non-chain atmosphere, Nakato is the place to visit. The staff is friendly and helpful. Hibachi chefs are funny and love posing for pictures. Hibachi choices are standard combination of two of the following: Shrimp, Chicken, Steak, Scallops. If sushi is preferred, it is also on the menu. Some sample sushi rolls are the Negihama and White Kelp. The Negihama roll, contains yellowtail and green onion, is simple yet full of taste and texture. The White Kelp roll is stuffed with chopped crab tempura, green onions, caviar and aioli, wrapped in white kelp. The large seating areas, especially Hibachi tables lend themselves to a terrific option for a birthday celebration with a large group. If you are feeling like a big spender, get the Japanese Wagyu Steak for $100. Parking is valet only. $$$

New York Prime Monarch Tower, 3424 Peachtree Rd., Atlanta, GA 30326; (404) 846-0644 www.newyorkprime.com

Located near the ritzy hotels near Lenox is New York Prime. All Steaks Are USDA Prime, hence the name. They are always aged 28 days and prepared with a charred exterior. If you like New York Strip, get the namesake. Note that they allow cigar smoking, so may not be the best choice for those with sensitivities. $$$$

Ninos 1931 Cheshire Bridge Rd., Atlanta, GA 30324; (404) 874-6505 www.ninosatlanta.com

Nino's is rather small, but very cozy. Another restaurant that has been in Atlanta for decades, it serves up authentic Italian cuisine. Their Bruschetta, Escargot and Calamari are all pretty tasty. The lasagna is classic and the ultimate in comfort food at Nino's. It comes overflowing with cheesy goodness and filled with meat. As one would expect, the selection of wines by the glass is very solid. Servers tend to push veal dishes, but Seafood dishes are much better. After your meal, they'll bring the dessert cart by. So, don't forget to save room, as many desserts are dreamy and made in house. Tiramisu, Coconut Cake, Bailey's Cheesecake, are just some of the desserts worth mentioning. Note: Although this is in the Buckhead area, this side of town is slightly seedy (read: neon-lit gentleman's clubs). $$$$

Ok Café 1284 W. Paces Ferry Rd., Atlanta, GA 30327; (404) 233-2888   www.okcafe.com

Located in the heart of Buckhead, this popular brunch spot is always hopping. Diners don't seem to mind the long waits for a table. Pancakes and omelets are favorite menu items. Although they are known for their breakfast foods, there are also a lot of Southern foods on the menu. Think Chicken fried steak, Collard Greens and Mac N Cheese. Portions are huge. The dining room is kitschy and the server's uniforms are all old school, like 1950s old school. Complete your retro dining experience with a burger and a milkshake (yes, they are wonderful and worth the money). Tip: Bypass the wait for a table and just sit at the counter. It is a freestanding building in a strip mall, so there is plenty of free parking all around. $$

Painted Pin 737 Miami Cir., Atlanta, GA 30324; (404) 814-8736 www.thepaintedpin.com

Looking for some adult gaming? Look no further than the upscale Painted Pin. With several gaming areas, the best is the bowling with comfy seats and table service. Get fried oysters and waffle dogs to munch on while you bowl. Tacos have a variety of fillings and come in trios. It's a terrific choice for an adult birthday party. Darts, skeeball and other nostalgic games are available in a convivial atmosphere. Note that the environment is not kid friendly. $$

Portofino 3199 Paces Ferry Pl., Atlanta, GA 30305; (404) 231-1136 www.portofinobistro.com

Portofino is tucked away from the main drag of Buckhead. No matter, it still has a lively crowd especially on weekends. Inside, the tables are set close together in this renovated house. When busy, the noise level can get quite high, so might not be the best setting for a romantic date on a Saturday night. Short rib Bruschetta appetizer should not be missed. The bread is piled high and heavy with meat.

The Fried Artichokes are a solid vegetarian choice, served up with a Tarragon aioli and are a secret menu item. They have seasonal specials like pumpkin items in the fall worth visiting for. They also do a fabulous brunch with lamb and Caviar atop potato pancakes. Reservations required. Note that even with reservations, patio seating is first come, first serve. $$$

Ray's on the River 6700 Powers Ferry Rd., Sandy Springs, GA 30339; (770) 955-1187 www.raysrestaurants.com

This beautiful restaurant overlooks the serene setting of Atlanta's Chattahoochee River. The outside is landscaped perfectly and makes for good photo ops. The pristine setting is also a top choice for rehearsal dinners. The divers menu offers seafood, and prime cuts of steak. Start dinner with the BBQ Shrimp and Crab Cakes (hands down some of the best in the city). Seafood is flown in daily and the signature dish is the Horseradish Crusted Grouper. Prime Rib lovers will enjoy the slow roasted cut of meat, available in twelve, sixteen and twenty ounce varieties. It is also one of the most in demand brunch spots in the area, offering nearly 80 selections including a carving station, peel and eat jumbo shrimp, a made to order omelet stations and an assortment of house made desserts. Reservations recommended. $$$$

Red Martini   3179 Peachtree Rd., Atlanta, GA 30305; (404) 254-3519   www.redmartiniatlanta.com

The dimly lit lounge is perfect for cozying up to your date. Red Martini has a large bar spanning much of the restaurant. There are signature cocktails and martinis, reasonably priced. Get the Red Rose, made with St. Germain, Gin, rosewater and muddled cucumber - a terrific balance, sweet, tart and boozy. A must order is the Red Martini Roll, made with Ahi Tuna, Snapper, Crab, Halibut, this roll has it all. Like it spicy? Get the Salmon Habanero Roll made with asparagus, salmon and goat cheese and an orange habanero aioli. $$$

The Red Snapper 2100 Cheshire Bridge Road, Atlanta, GA 30324;   (404) 634-8947 www.redsnapperatlanta.com

Don't go to Red Snapper for the décor, go for the delicious seafood options that have been pleasing customers for about three decades. Overlooking the somewhat seedy surroundings, this place has some spectacular seafood, especially if you like Red Snapper. You've never seen so many different ways that Snapper could be prepared! The Ginger Snapper is especially lovely. There's a Thai influence in many of their dishes as well, since the owner is Thai. They do grow some of their herbs in the yard like Thai Basil. Get he coconut cake for dessert. Tip: They make an excellent Gumbo too! $$$

Restaurant Eugene 2277 Peachtree Rd., Atlanta, GA 30309; (404) 355-0321 www.restauranteugene.com

Named for his grandfather, Restaurant Eugene is owned by Linton Hopkins. Hopkins was a James Beard nominee for Best Chef: Southeast 2011. They are extremely big on the farm to table movement here. The food and topnotch service leaves nothing to be desired, but it is very pricey. Portions aren't huge, but the creativity and complexity of each dish makes each bite worth the price tag. Melt in your mouth Salmon and Crispy Duck are two mains not to be missed. Five and Seven course tasting menus are offered. $$$$

Rock N Taco 3247 Roswell Rd, Atlanta, GA 30305; (404) 841-1048 www.rockntacoatl.com

With a live band on many evenings, this spot makes for a good spot for an inexpensive meet up with friends. Prime seating is on the rooftop bar. Start with the Ceviche, made

with shrimp and large chunks of lobster, a generous portion. The highlight of the menu is the gourmet tacos with a variety of 20 to choose from. Unique ones include the Duck Confit, Roasted Lamb and Tuna Poke. Fajitas are huge and enough to feed an army. $$

Saltyard 1820 Peachtree St., Atlanta, GA 30309; (404) 382-8088 www.saltyardatlanta.com

Who says tapas are just for Spanish foods? Not the folks behind Saltyard. The lively atmosphere right of Peachtree Road is perfect for a group gathering. Don't miss out on the Shrooms on Toast, which is so popular it never leaves the menu. Fried Brussels are good options, as are the seafood options, which do change regularly. Skip brunch as the dishes aren't as good as dinner. $$$

Seven Lamps 3400 Around Lenox, Atlanta, GA 30305; (404) 467-8950 www.sevenlampsatl.com

Though this spot can be tough to find unless you know where to look, it is worth seeking out. It is located in the strip mall off Peachtree Road that is between Lenox Mall and the W Hotel. Seating is mostly communal, so good for groups, but don't forget to make reservations. Cocktails are a star here. Don't miss out on specialty pastas, Mortadella Macarons or the secret menu item: 50 / 50 burger. $$$

SOHO 4300 Paces Ferry Rd., Atlanta, GA 30339; (770) 801-0069 www.sohoatlanta.com

Tucked away in the Vinings Jubilee shopping center, SOHO has been impressing Vinings residents and hosting business dinners for about two decades. Start with the Salmon Thai or a Wagyu Carpaccio. For entrees get the Elk Tenderloin, the raspberry / mustard sauce compliments it perfectly with a side of heavenly sweet potato gratin. A Chilean Seabass served with Forbidden rice is outstanding as well. There's also a gluten free menu and pre-theatre dining menu. $$$$

Souper Jenny 130 West Paces Ferry Rd., Atlanta GA, 30305; (404) 239-9023 www.souperjennyatl.com

The décor is eclectic. The varieties of soups change daily so as not to bore anyone. The Turkey chili is one of the most popular menu items. Other soups that are favored are the gazpacho, cucumber (served cold) or chicken tortilla. They offer a lunch special that includes your choice of selections. They are located in the Atlanta History Center, so get cultured before or after your lunch. $

Southern Art At the Intercontinental Hotel, 3315 Peachtree Rd., Atlanta, GA 30326; (404) 946-9070 www.southernart.com

Located in the Intercontinental Hotel, the restaurant gets its name from Chef Art Smith. Passing by the charcuterie station when you walk in, you'll be tempted by the many options of this "Ham Bar" (various ham options). Though the menu changes seasonally, items like Oxtail and Pork can usually be found on it. The upscale southern cuisine is complimented by the lovely décor including art displaying on the ceiling. $$$

Southern Gentleman 3035 Peachtree Rd., Atlanta, GA 30305; (404) 939-9845 www.thesoutherngentlemanatl.com

The Shoppes at Buckhead Atlanta has certainly impressed Atlantans with the sheer décor of the restaurants. A huge portrait of Mark Twain watches over diners at the Southern Gentlemen gastropub. The restaurant features killer cocktails and serves up southern dishes in their classic southern serve ware. Starters like the shrimp corn dogs and boudin balls with hot pepper jelly, are quite enjoyable and outshine entrees. $$$

St. Cecilia 3455 Peachtree Rd., Atlanta, GA 30326; (404) 554-9995   www.stceciliaatl.com

Restaurateur Ford Fry seems to have taken Atlanta by storm and there seems to be no shortage of cuisine he hasn't conquered. St. Cecilia is his upscale spin on Italian / Mediterranean fare. The vibe is Manhattan with a bustling bar scene making patrons wait for a table despite reservations. Portions are quite small but complex. Lobster ravioli and Octopus are outstanding here. Great cocktail and wine options abound. $$$$

Storico Fresco 3167 Peachtree Rd., Atlanta, GA 30305; (404) 500-2181   www.storicofresco.com

What was once a small shop only offering pastas to go, has turned into a full-fledged restaurant. Squid Ink Pasta? Check. Chickpea pasta. Check. Stop in and pick up a delicious dinner to go. Guests can't seem to get enough of the lasagna. Dining in? A Zucchini carpaccio is lovely as are the meatballs as a starter. Sausage pasta is incredible, but they do more than that. A seafood entrée has prawns, and Snapper, lightly fried. Desserts are very creative and light. $$$

Tomo 3630 Peachtree Rd #140, Atlanta, GA 30326; (404) 835-2708 www.tomorestaurant.com/

Run by chef Tom Naito, a native of Japan, came to the United States to study and has worked in New York Boston, and even at Las Vegas at the prestigious NoBu Restaurant. After learning from master Nobu Matsuhisa, Tom has begun his own style at Tomo. Mixing his training in the art of French and Italian cooking in to his Japanese offerings, dishes are like a work of art. For lunch order the bento box with Chef's choice sushi. At dinner, start with the Hamachi Sashimi or the Usuzurkuri (Fluke Sashimi) which comes with cilantro and sriracha sauce. Specials the Sea Urchin wrapped in seaweed, don't disappoint. Staff is adept at making recommendations and steering those who are unsure of what to order in the right direction. Reservations recommended. Closed Sundays. $$$

True Food Kitchen 3393 Peachtree Rd., Atlanta, GA 30326; (404) 481-2980 www.truefoodkitchen.com

Located at Lenox Square Mall, this healthy eating spot is perfect to enjoy without any guilt. Salads and salmon and light shrimp pasta are tasty, yet won't hurt your waistline. They also make many house "elixirs" that are quite refreshing. Think Pomegranite limeade. But you can booze it up if you want to with a Ginger Margarita. Though everything is tasty, the price tag can be quite steep. $$$

Valenza 1441 Dresden Dr. Ste 100, Atlanta, GA 30319; (404) 969-3233   www.valenzarestaurant.com

Along with its sister restaurant, Haven, this is popular with the many residents of the Brookhaven community. They do have a solid wine selection, plus they make their own limoncello in house. The mussels, which are also available at Haven, are a standout, garlicky with chunks of tomatoes. For mains the Risotto is prepared creamy and al dente, just as it should be. Vegetarians and non-vegetarians can both appreciate the butternut squash ravioli, with its pecans, brown butter and sage. The Pork saltimbocca is tender, juicy, and tasty. Service is very attentive here. The restaurant works well for a cozy date or a girl's night out and is regularly host to birthday celebrations. $$$$

Varasano's Pizza 2171 Peachtree Rd., Atlanta, GA 30309; (404) 352-8216   www.varasanos.com

An almost overnight sensation, Varasano's creator and owner, Jeff Varasano, a former techie, started making pizzas here in the Neapolitan way. This style is cooking pizzas for only a couple minutes in a very high degree oven. Since opening, Varasano's has had a loyal following of customers. Patrons can build their own pizza by selecting ingredients of their choosing. Nana's, the house special, is the pizza his grandmother used to make, topped with mozzarella and tomato sauce with a secret blend of Italian herbs. For something different, try the New Haven Clam: made with Clams, Mussels and Garlic; it can be ordered with white or red sauce. $$

Vero Pizzeria 1441 Dresden Drive #120, Brookhaven, GA 30319; (404) 869-1166 www.vero-pizzeria.com

The word "vero" is an Italian word that translates to "true" in English. Stacks of imported Italian flour line the doorway to Vero Pizzeria. Butcher-block tables, wood shelving and tile give the restaurant an Italian rustic charm. Fresh herbs hang on a converted shabby chic chandelier. The focal point of the restaurant is its gigantic, 6,800 pound pizza oven, imported from Italy. One pie is good enough for two to split. Get the Meatball or 'Njuda spreadable sausage pies. A Super Tuscan pairs nicely with these. $$$

Vine & Tap 2770 Lenox Rd., Atlanta, GA 30324; (404) 600-5820 www.vineandtapatl.com

The gorgeous space is trendy and begs you to forget you are in a strip mall. Husband and wife team behind it, Ian and Susan are huge oenophiles, having tasted each wine they stock, and there are plenty. Surprisingly, the prices are very reasonable. Crab cakes, charcuterie with locally sourced meats and a NY Strip are all impressive. There's also a private room for events. Tip: They have oyster happy hour. Check the site for details. $$$

Watershed 1820 Peachtree St., Atlanta, GA 30309; (404) 809-3561 www.watershedrestaurant.com

Owned by one of the famed Indigo Girls, Watershed is a must visit for anyone wanting classic southern dishes minus the folksy atmosphere. There's a gorgeous oak bar that was crafted from a single oak tree. Sip on a glass of vino and treat yourself to some apps if dining solo. Executive chef, Zeb Stevenson is a noted chef around Atlanta and was even a Chopped Television show winner. Tip: Wednesday nights feature some of the best fried chicken in the city. But it is only available that night until it's gone. $$$

Yebo Beach Haus   111 West Paces Ferry Rd., Atlanta, GA 30305; (404) 869-1992   www.yebobeachhaus.com

Many Atlantans often lament that the only thing Atlanta is missing is a beach. While this spot doesn't offer a beach, it certainly has a beachy feel. And with tasty South African influenced dishes, it may just make your longing for a beach subside, if only for a bit. Get the Biltong, a kind of South African beef jerky to start. Then order some tapas like the Bobotie Bunny Chow, Prawn Tacos or Ostrich Sliders. $$

Zinburger   3393 Peachtree Rd. NE #3065A, Atlanta, GA 30326; (404) 963-9611 www.zinburgereast.com

All burgers are either CAB (certified angus beef) or American Kobe. An Ahi Tuna salad is divine too. The hardest decision you may have at Zinburger isn't choosing which salad, or even which burger you will have. It is which pile of fried goodness you will indulge in: Zucchini fries, Double Truffle fries or Onion rings. Truffles are imported on a weekly basis for the fries. Get the El Diablo burger and top it off with a milkshake - Bananas Foster, Strawberry Cheesecake and more or Salted Caramel. $$

CHAPTER 3
Downtown

Downtown includes Cabbagetown, Castleberry Hill, East Atlanta, Grant Park and Edgewood. For many years, Downtown Atlanta was a mecca for businesses and conventioneers and not much else. At night, it was deserted, many leaving for their homes in the suburbs. In the last couple years, there has been a resurgence in the popularity of in-town living. With it, there's been more condo development and as would be expected, an upswing in restaurants populating the downtown area.

Agave Restaurant 242 Boulevard SE, Atlanta, GA 30312; (404) 588-0006 www.agaverestaurant.com

The unique interior of this restaurant is reminiscent of an old Spanish Church. The cuisine is upscale Southwestern. Seafood lovers who happen to also enjoy Mexican will especially appreciate the menu here. Start with a Jalapeno margarita and fried lobster tail. The restaurant is known for its Cayenne Chicken Breast and it is one of the most popular dishes on the menu along with the spicy Tequila Anejo Shrimp. It can get very crowded, so reservations are a must. Tip: All entrees are $12 between 5 and 6 pm. $$$

Alma Cocina – 191 Peachtree St Atlanta, GA 30303;
(404) 968-9662 www. Alma-atlanta.com

It's a beacon of light in a sea of chain restaurants. The menu is
divided into categories of appetizers, ceviches, soups / salads,
plates, taquitos, Huaraches, sides, desserts. Huaraches are a
must at this downtown Latin restaurant. They are crisp corn
masas with different toppings. A goat or shrimp is wonderful. Ceviches are all winners as well. Rather than individually
ordering, lots of small plates for sharing like tapas are the
way to go. $$

Ann Snack Bar 1615 Memorial Dr Atlanta, GA 30317;
(404) 687-9207

Long before burgers and hot dogs became hip and trendy,
Ann's Snack bar was serving them up. The trip to Ann's is as
much about the experience as it is about trying the famous
Ghetto Burger. You only enter if there are empty bar stools.
Sadly, Miss Ann passed away several years ago but her legacy

lives on. Don't come here in a hurry or on a lunch hour. The Ghetto burger is a monstrosity – two patties not one. Even for those who come "hangry" it is a still a feat to finish the entire thing. Cash only. $

Argosy 470 Flat Shoals Ave SE, Atlanta, GA 30316; (404) 577-0407 www.argosy-east.com

Grab a seat on the indoor balcony overlooking the lower level of this East Atlanta gastropub. Nosh on small plates like Togarashi Popcorn, Steamed Duck Buns and Beef Poutine. Cocktails like the Navigator with gin and lavender syrup perfectly compliment these upscale bar bites. Creative items like Japanese Oyster Soup and Carrot-Parsnip fries but the Plancha Burger is a customer favorite. Specials happen often, so you'll never bore with the menu and the playful chef creations like Landlocked-Gumbo with chicken and andouille sausage. $$

Atlanta Grill (Ritz-Carlton) 181 Peachtree Street Atlanta, GA 30303; (404) 659 0400 www.ritzcarlton.com/en/hotels/georgia/atlanta/dining

Worth it for a splurge or when celebrating a special occasion, the Atlanta Grill will spoil you with its downright Southern hospitality and exquisite food. Although the décor inside is beautiful, seating outside is where all the action is. Sit perched several stories above the hustle and bustle of the streets of downtown Atlanta. Watch the action below as you sit nestled in your nook. The menu isn't huge, but has some standouts. Steaks and seafood are prepared flawlessly, as one would expect. Staff works together to provide an outstanding meal and experience, all while making it seem effortless. $$$$

Bottle Rocket 180 Walker St. Atlanta, GA 30313; (404) 574-5680 www.bottlerocketatl.com

Situated rather close to the central downtown area in close proximity to downtown attractions, but just far enough off the beaten path that visitors wouldn't know it is there is Bottle Rocket. The small bar /restaurant is full of bold colors and personality and has a crowd of loyal regulars. It is the modern day version of *Cheers* of downtown Atlanta. Drinks are extremely well-made with high end ingredients but at reasonable prices. The focus is mainly on sushi, with some other cooked items thrown in the mix. The tuna burger with the slightest bit of panko is a highlight. Tip: They offer regular sushi classes (see pictures above). $$

Delia's Chicken and Sausage 881 Marietta St, Atlanta, GA 30318; (404) 254-0408 www.thesausagestand.com

Who would have thought that chicken sausages could become a craze? However, since opening, Delia's has been wowing guests with their unique chicken sausage varieties. For truly Southern, get the Smack N Cheese with macaroni and cheese, collard greens and comeback sauce. Or get three sliders, especially the Chorizo topped with Pimento cheese. They also do breakfast and are open 24 hours on the weekends. $

Der Biergarten 300 Marietta St. Northwest, Atlanta, GA 30313; (404) 521-2728 www.derbiergarten.com

Make every attempt to dine in the beer garden, the restaurant's namesake. They've done everything possible to make this biergarten as authentic as possible. The beer selection

is wide, but they've kept the pricing rather reasonable. Begin with the giant pretzel, which is enough to feed 2 or 3 and comes with a variety of mustard dipping sauces. Main entrée highlights are the Wiener schnitzel or Jagerschnitzel. Tip: They validate parking for 3 hours, so no need to rush through diner. Plus the patio is dog friendly. $$

Dua Vietnamese 53 Broad St Atlanta, GA 30303; (404) 589-8889 www.yougotpho.com

A favorite of downtown workers and students, Dua can get extremely crowded at lunch, with a line out the door. But the staff moves quickly and patrons can get their meals in 5 – 10 minutes. It is not uncommon for items to sell out as they get fresh deliveries each day. The Pho is certainly not to be missed, whether you choose beef or chicken. Mi Xao (Stir fried noodles) and Com Bo Luc Lac (rice with shaking beef) and Lemongrass tofu are other highlights. Note: They close at 5 weekdays and 4 Friday and Saturday, so are not open for dinner and are closed Sundays. $

El Myr 1091 Euclid Ave Atlanta, GA 30307; (404) 588-0250 www.elmyr.com

El Myr is located in the Little Five Points neighborhood, an artsy and eclectic neighborhood that draw in a crowd and staff with tattoos and piercings. This is a true dive bar, but the burritos are so hefty and delicious, it becomes easy to overlook the atmosphere. The margaritas are strong and tasty. Interesting burritos are the Pad Thai or Tofu burrito. There are lots of vegetarian options like the potato, corn and black olive burrito. The patio is wonderful for chilling with friends on a warm spring day. Extras: they are open late night and have a juke box with a good music selection. $

Elliot Street Pub 51 Elliott St Atlanta, GA 30313; (404) 523-2174 www.elliottstreet.com

This pub is teeny tiny, but huge on hospitality and friend-liness. As is usual with the Castleberry Hill neighborhood, it definitely has a regular crowd and they populate this bar most nights but weekend nights can prove especially difficult to snag a spot. The small menu is mostly deli-style sandwiches but they are made from scratch and extreme-ly tasty. Roast beef and Cheddar on Ciabatta is a popular sandwich. For a twist on Pastrami, try the Greek Pastrami with feta cheese and tzatziki sauce. The beer selection is huge, and as more flows, the party often spills out onto the street. $

Fox Brothers BBQ 1238 Dekalb Ave Atlanta, GA 30307; (404) 577-4030 www.foxbrosbbq.com

Arguably some of the best BBQ in the city, Fox Brothers BBQ, was open for little time before it exploded in its popularity. It is truly a mecca for fried foods. For starters the fried pickles and the fried ribs are top choices for appetizers. For wing lovers, the smoked wings are a must try. The overall smoky, sweet and citrus flavors come through and meld perfectly with the moist meat underneath the skin. Ribs and pulled pork are tremendous. So is the burger: chopped brisket, pimiento cheese plus a couple strips of bacon. Southern favorites like Collard Greens and Black eyed peas are done perfectly. Don't forget to try the Burnt Ends and if you are feeling adventurous try the Frito pie. Tip: While there isn't much parking in the front of the building to be found, it can easily be found on the side streets. $$

Gato 1660 McLendon Ave Atlanta, GA 30307; (404) 371-0889

Only open until 2:30 pm, don't expect dinner here but do expect to find yummy meals, friendly service in this small space. Sweet Potato Pancakes are a reason alone to make this place a brunch destination. Omelets and Huevos Rancheros are the highlight of the menu. Sit at the bar if you're dining solo or only two in your party if you'd prefer to be seated immediately. Otherwise, be prepared for a short wait for a table. $

Grindhouse Killer Burgers 209 Edgewood Ave Atlanta, GA 30303; (404) 522-3444   www.grindhouseburgers.com

Grindhouse had humble beginnings in the Sweet Auburn Curb Market, but has expanded to several locations in Atlanta including the Airport. However, this location is special. The market is part of a large shopping area. Burgers are ground fresh and served medium, well done upon request. Guests can build their own burger or choose from the Grindhouse burgers. The Apache which comes with pepper jack cheese and New Mexico chiles is a great choice for a slightly spicy burger. The Yankee, with bacon and blue cheese is another good choice. The sweet potato kettle chips are fresh cut and spice dusted. $

Gunshow 924 Garrett St, Atlanta, GA 30316; (404) 380-1886
www.gunshowatl.com

Spoiler Alert: Part of the experience of going to Gunshow is not knowing exactly what to expect. It's dim sum but with American food and there are multiple chefs? **Yes.** Besides the loud dining room (it's one big room with community seating), there's continual interruption from the chefs. Not the best spot for an intimate dinner. Chefs present their dishes to each table to be accepted or rejected. Items include Lobster rolls, Squid Ink Calamari, and Smoked Pork Loin. Prices are vastly different and really not based on the quality or quantity of food, so it can be hit or miss. Skip the lackluster wine in favor of the delicious cocktails. $$$

Gus's Fried Chicken The Mall at Peachtree Center, 231 W Peachtree St A-05, Atlanta, GA 30303; (404) 996-2837 www.gusfriedcihcken.com

Hailing from Memphis, is some of the best fried chicken in the Southeast United States. Find them at the Peachtree Center Mall food court right off the MARTA line. They can be tricky to find as you must go downstairs from the main food court. If you want fried everything you can certainly find it at Gus's with starters of fried pickles, tomatoes and okra. However, the star and the main reason for coming here is the fried chicken. They use fresh never frozen chicken and fry in peanut oil. Don't expect fast food prices, but as an indulgence once in a while, it's so worth it. $$

Holy Taco 1314 Glenwood Ave Atlanta, GA 30316; (404) 230-6177 www.holy-taco.com

Another gem in the East Atlanta Village, Holy Taco fits the bill for adventurous eaters. Chicken Heart and Beef Tongue tacos can all be found here. Unless starving, two tacos are enough satisfy any appetite. Other menu highlights include the Pozole, Chilaquiles, and Roasted Corn on The Cobb. The organic margaritas are highly addictive, but watch out as they can sneak up on you. The menu is seasonal and does change often. Although it is a casual spot, it is somewhat of a hybrid between American Mexican and Authentic Mexican, so don't expect free chips and salsa. When it gets crowded, it can be extremely noisy but a super people watching spot. $$

Homegrown 968 Memorial Drive, Atlanta, GA 30316; (404) 222-0455 www.homegrownga.com

They've won lots of awards for having the best breakfast for the Comfy Chicken Biscuit which is swimming in gravy and served with a side of grits. However, the Lynne Stack - 2 salmon patties, 2 fried green tomatoes, sautéed spinach, and tomatoes, with melted pimento is just as good an entrée. Because of the fame, expect very long waits on weekends. However, if you are a non-southerner looking to try grits for the first time, this is a great choice. $

Le Petite Marche 1984 Hosea L. Williams Drive Atlanta, GA 30317; (404) 371-9888   www.leptitmarche.net

This Kirkwood spot serves breakfast all day, every day and is open from 8 am to 5 pm. You can build your own biscuit starting at just $5. The menu also includes varied sandwiches like a jerk chicken or shrimp po boy. The most popular item is the Grits Stack - Creamy grits topped with scrambled eggs, cheddar, marinated shrimp and bacon. Everything is reasonably priced at $10 or less. $

Lotta Frutta 590 Auburn Ave Atlanta, GA 30312; (404) 588-0857 www.lottafrutta.com

One of the most unique and popular restaurants in the downtown area is Lotta Frutta. Since opening, customers haven't stopped singing its praises. They focus on fresh fruit cups and smoothies and vegetarian sandwiches. However, carnivores love it too. It is the perfect fix for when you want something substantial but not meaty or greasy. Get the Dolce Vitta fruit cup, which is fruit topped with vanilla yogurt, granola and honey. Sandwiches are served on sweet Latin bread, which is pressed panini-style. The Just Veggin' is a highlight with Havarti cheese and fresh vegetables. During the winter don't miss out on the tasty soups. Tip: Inca Cola (a Peruvian favorite) is served here. $

The Mercury Ponce City Market 675 Ponce De Leon Ave, Atlanta, GA 30308; (404) 500-5253 www.themercuryatl.com

"Inspired by the culture of the 1960s" is how The Mercury describes itself. Think cocktails like Manhattans, Old Fashioneds, Martinis, Mai Tais and steak dinners. Open for both lunch and dinner, you can save money by day drinking with your lunch. Though steak is highlight here, especially Prime Rib, they mostly serve sandwiches at lunch. So, if you want to really go big, visit for dinner. $$$

Nick's Food to Go 240 Martin Luther King Jr Dr Atlanta, GA 30312; (404) 521-2220 www.nicksfood.com

Colorful murals decorate the walls outside this Greek spot. Nick's serves up some of the best gyros in town. A gyro order + Greek fries is enough to feed two. The fries are worthy trying as they are truly unique. Fries are potato wedges fried and sprinkled with lemon juice, oregano served with tzatziki sauce. Notable dishes when available are the Greek Lasagna (Pastitsio) and the Moussaka. Note: There are no tables inside – Take-Out only. Closed Sundays. $

No Mas 180 Walker St Atlanta, GA 30313; (404) 574-5678
www.nomascantina.com

It is the décor that is the draw to this downtown restaurant. The two story restaurant is outfitted in a colorful Mexican vibe. The salsa has overall unique smoky flavor that is delicious. Chicken Enchiladas with Guajillo Sauce are tasty. Since it is a large place it is a good choice for groups. Note that service can be slow when it is busy. $$

Panbury's Double Crust Pies 231 Peachtree St Atlanta, GA 30303; (404) 600-8354 www.panburys.com

These savory pies are just the fix for those craving comfort food. Located in the Peachtree Center food court, it is a perfect stop for a snack if you find yourself downtown or taking MARTA from the airport. From behind the counter, the pies look deceptively small. Just beware, Panbury's pies are very filling and full of hearty ingredients. The two best are the Country Chicken and the Black Pepper Beef. Panbury's Beef pie is made with braised beef shoulder in a rich brandy sauce. There were thick slices of beef in this pie, not just ground beef . And the Country Chicken pie? Not sure if it is the leeks or the tarragon cream sauce, but I'd file this under foodgasm for sure. $

Paschal's 180 Northside Dr SW #B, Atlanta, GA 30313; (404) 525-2023 www.paschalsatlanta.com

If you want to experience something with historical significance, visit Paschal's in Castleberry Hill. Since 1947, James and Robert Paschal, the founders of Atlanta's historic Paschal's Restaurant, have been serving the Atlanta community. During the 1960s, they became very involved in the Civil Rights movement. Paschal's became a meeting place for civil rights leaders like Martin Luther King, Jr. Begin your evening with The Legacy cocktail, a key ingredient being sweet tea. This is the south, after all. Order the enormous fried chicken and end your meal with Peach Cobbler. $$

Polaris 265 Peachtree St NE, Atlanta, GA 30303; (404) 460-6425 www.hyatt.com/corporate/restaurants/ Polaris/en/Polaris.html

High atop the Hyatt Regency in downtown Atlanta is the much famed Blue Dome or Polaris. Not only does the Polaris make their own Bourbon (start your dinner with a Manhattan), but they make their own honey and grow many of their own herbs. While you are rotating 25 stories above Peachtree Street, you can glimpse the bee garden on the top of the International Tower. Executive Chef Rodney Ashley keeps the menu small and changes it quite often. Think items like Grouper cheeks and spicy jumbo shrimp with Asian vegetables. The Steak Oscar, however, is so popular it never leaves the menu. Tip: Try to make your dinner reservation to coincide with the sunset for optimal view. $$$$

Poor Calvin's 510 Piedmont Ave, Atlanta, GA 30308; (404) 254-4051 www.poorcalvins.com

Located in an unassuming remodeled home in downtown, you would probably pass right by Poor Calvin's without giving it a second thought, but you'd be missing out on

some outstanding fusion food. Owner Calvin Phan, serves up creative items like Frog's legs with Roti (and Indian bread) or Duck pate topped with pop rocks. There's a mix of classic cocktails and unique ones like the Frankly, My Dear with Gin and house made rosewater. Or get what is the best Pisco Sour you can find outside of Peru. $$$

Ray's in the City 240 Peachtree St, Atlanta, GA 30303; (404) 524-9224 www.raysrestaurannts.com.

With the popularity of Ray's on the River, the folks behind the successful restaurant decided that downtown shouldn't miss out on all the delicious seafood. The downtown spot features incredible options like whole roasted fish, lobster and even some sushi specialties. Save some money by visiting at lunch. $$$$

Ria's Bluebird 421 Memorial Dr Atlanta, GA 30312; (404) 521-3737 www.riasbluebird.com

Ria's is located directly across from an Atlanta Landmark, the Oakland Cemetery. It is somewhat of a funky atmosphere. The NY Times even rated them to have the "Best Pancakes." Business travelers who come to Atlanta regularly, have put Ria's on the must-visit each time. Shrimp and Grits and the Brisket Breakfast are also popular. Also don't miss out on trying the biscuits and gravy. The biscuits are light and fluffy, while the gravy is rich enough to make you forget there isn't any meat in it. They don't take reservations, so come prepared to wait on weekends. However, they are open every day from 8 am to 3 pm serving brunch. $

Reuben's Deli 57 Broad St NW Atlanta, GA 30303; (404) 589-9800 www.reubensdeliatlanta.com

Don't be put off by the long lines you'll see when you enter Reuben's, they move rather quickly. If you are craving a solid Reuben or really any New York deli style sandwich, this place is worth a visit. It is a pretty authentic New York experience as the staff has a slight attitude but it is part of the shtick of the New York vibe. You can't go wrong with the classic Reuben. A menu highlight is the Sera-wich which has Turkey, Greek Mayo, and Feta Cheese. So, is the New Yorker with Corned Beef, Pastrami and Cheese. Claudio, the owner, gets to know regular customers and is interested in making long-lasting customers. Tip: They deliver or you can call ahead and your order will be waiting for you when you arrive. Closed on Sundays. $

Shed at Glenwood 475 Bill Kennedy Way Atlanta, GA 30316; (404) 835-4363 www.theshedatglenwood.com

One of the first upscale restaurants on the Eastside, The Shed is an elegantly designed restaurant perfect for romantic evening or celebratory dinner. Charcuterie and oysters are delicious. They also have some intriguing pasta dishes. Sliders of many varieties are a hit here. In fact, they have a phenomenal deal on Wednesdays of giant sliders for just $3 each. They serve brunch late on weekends too if you find yourself in need of some hair of the dog relief. $$$

Six Feet Under 415 Memorial Dr Ste E Atlanta, GA 30312; (404) 523-6664 www.sixfeetunderatlanta.com

The restaurant, located across the street from a cemetery, is appropriately named. When the weather is nice, patrons fill the rooftop patio. Want to try something a little different? How about the Rat Toes (jalapeno stuffed shrimp wrapped in bacon)? Fried Green Tomatoes and Scallops and Grits are southern favorites that shouldn't be missed. You can't go wrong with shrimp, whether it is fried or blackened. The blackened catfish is delicious as well. Although the restaurant is primarily seafood based, their burger is quite good and is almost a hidden secret around Atlanta. Beer selection is plentiful. This is a fantastic end to a tour of the historic Oakland cemetery that sits across from the restaurant. They don't take reservations but do take call-ahead seating. $$

Smoke Ring 309 Nelson St, Atlanta, GA 30313; (404) 228-6377 www.smokeringatlanta.com

One thing downtown had been missing is a great barbecue restaurant and Smoke Ring came to the rescue. Some slow cooked meats exhibit a pink color just under the surface crust (called bark). This pink ring is referred to as a "smoke ring" hence the name. If you are feeling adventurous try the Boiled Peanut Martini. The upscale spot is designed with beautiful brick and reclaimed wood. Expect your typical barbecue plates, though sides like the Brussels sprouts with Maple Syrup and the Chipotle Corn on the Cobb are terrific. Tip: They also have smoked turkeys during Thanksgiving that guests rave about. $$

SoBa Vietnamese 560 Gresham Ave Atlanta, GA 30316; (404) 627-9911 soba-eav.com

SoBa is just off the main strip of the East Atlanta Village and is actually a refurbished house. Residents of the EAV appreciate the proximity of a Vietnamese spot which saves them from traversing to Buford Highway. Jack Fruit Martinis are the most popular drink ordered. Start your meal off with the steamed spring rolls, the dipping sauce that accompanies the rolls is lick-your-plate worthy. This Vietnamese restaurant is a fantastic restaurant to visit when in the mood for decent Pho. If Pho isn't your thing, they have lots of other tasty menu options. Try the grilled pork, smoky and crispy, the portion is huge. Sundays are medium bowl of Pho and Blood Mary for $12. $

Sun Dial 210 Peachtree St NW Atlanta, GA 30303; (404) 589-7506 www.sundialrestaurant.com

One of the most touristy places in Atlanta is the Sun Dial. This rotating restaurant / bar atop the Westin Hotel has spectacular views of the Atlanta Skyline. Service is solid. The food is tasty and beautifully presented, but isn't the most innovative out there. Think steaks, pasta and fish. The atmosphere is certainly perfect for a romantic evening or special occasion. On the floor above, you can see lots of historic memorabilia and learn interesting facts about Atlanta. Note that this floor doesn't revolve. It is definitely a place to take an out-of-towner to impress them with the views of the city. $$$$

The Porter Beer Bar 1156 Euclid Ave Atlanta, GA 30307; (404) 223-0393 www.theporterbeerbar.com

The Porter is located in Little Five Points, a small, artsy neighborhood near Downtown. Entering the Porter, you'd be surprised how tiny it is, but the space is oddly laid out in that it stretches far back and wraps around to form an "L" shape. The beer menu is one of the most extensive in Atlanta with beer pairing suggestions accompany menu items. At first glance, many might dismiss this gastropub as a dive bar and skip the food. But dishes are inventive and high on flavor. Specials have included Duck Prosciutto and Vindaloo Ravioli. Don't forget to give the fries and hush puppies a try as well. The hush puppies with bacon and a Fuji apple dipping sauce are a nice twist on a classic southern side. Tip: There is free parking around the back of the restaurant. $$

Thumbs Up Diner 573 Edgewood Ave NE Atlanta, GA 30312; (404) 223-0690 www.thumbsupdiner.com

Reasonable pricing and consistent food is what you'll find at Thumb's Up Diner. Menu highlights are the French Toast made with Challah and Sassy Scramble which are eggs with cream cheese Want a skillet breakfast that comes with everything mixed up? Try "The Heap," which comes with home fries, eggs and cheese and just about anything else you'd like added. For picky eaters, it is nice that their breakfasts are customizable, which they call the Build Your Own Breakfast. So, you could order two eggs with cheese and a pancake with spuds (home fries). Tip: Don't miss out on their jams. Rather than store bought jams, theirs are house made. Note that payment is cash only. Waits can be very long on weekends. $

Trader Vic's Hilton Atlanta, 255 Courtland St, Atlanta, GA 30303; (404) 221-6339 www. tradervicsatl.com

What once was old is new again. Though the tiki theme had lost popularity, it seems revived and Trader Vic's is excellent tiki fare. From the décor and aptly attired servers, the island drinks and music will get you dancing and the food will delight. Located in the Atlanta Hilton, it is a terrific choice if you are doing a staycation or want to plan a fun dinner for your kids. $$$

Vortex 438 Moreland Ave Atlanta, GA 30307; (404) 688-1828 www.thevortexbarandgrill.com

Enter through the large skull to the main dining area of the Vortex. Once inside, choose from a selection of burgers. The bacon and blue is terrific. So is the Cowboy Burger with ham and bbq sauce. But if you really want the ultimate burger (the one that was featured on Man vs. Food) order the Coronary Bypass, 1/2lb burger, 3 slices of cheese, 4 strips of bacon, and a fried egg to top. Skip the fries and order the much better tater tots. There are a ton of beer choices and they have a fully stocked bar too. Part of the gimmick of the Vortex is that the servers here have a small attitude. It isn't rudeness, but if you are expecting a place where the servers fall all over you, this isn't it. They do allow smoking here. Tip: free dinner on your birthday. $$

White Oak Kitchen & Cocktails 270 Peachtree St Atlanta, GA 30303; (404) 524-7200

The bright restaurant features delicious southern cuisine from notable chef Todd Richards. Cocktails come with playful names like Ryed in the Streetcar, Dimming of the Day and Follow Your Bliss. Try the smoked pork chop, thick and glazed with apple cider, a standout dish. Southern starters like Pimento cheese fritters and watermelon salad with pickles watermelon rind don't disappoint. White Oak Kitchen & Cocktails is a terrific spot to take out of town guests for a meal when you are taking in the downtown activities. $$$

Wrecking Bar 292 Moreland Ave, Atlanta, GA 30307; (404) 221-2600 www.wreckingbarbrewpub.com

If you like architecture and brews, you'll want to visit Wrecking Bar. This gorgeous historic building has been preserved and turned into a cool gastropub. They have elegant cocktails and killer beer list. Think items like duck tacos or brisket for entrees. The staff is pleasant and knowledgeable. Tip: If you are into quirky places, this is a neat spot for a private event. $$

Ziba's Bistro 560 Boulevard SE, Atlanta, GA 30312; (404) 622-4440 www.zibasbistro.com

Ziba's Bistro is a small restaurant that serves up tapas and a great selection of wine. The atmosphere is very laid back and casual – no need to get dressed up. Start with the Flatbread or Hummus, if you are having a full meal. However, the highlight of this spot is the mussels and the half a dozen different sauces you can get with them. The white or red sauce is super, but my recommendation is the Turmeric with cumin, smoked paprika, cayenne pepper, coconut milk. It comes with a huge portion of fries too, making for a very filling meal. $$

CHAPTER 4
Inman Park /
Virginia Highland /
Old Fourth Ward

These neighborhoods have received radical transformation and gentrification in the last decade. Once thought to be on the decline, it has seen resurgence in the last handful of years. Some very high-end restaurants have established themselves are really helped to anchor the neighborhood.

Ammazza – 591 Edgewood Ave, Atlanta, GA 30312; (404) 228-1036 www.ammazza.com

Get the Ammazzare with sausage, peppers onions and basil. It's glorious, but the Bolognese with meatballs and sausage is a tad better, probably because of the addition of Ricotta cheese. Even with sausage + meatballs it is well balanced, each bite not overly meaty. Like spicy? Get the Inferno with spicy Sopressata and calabrian peppers. One pie could easily feed three or four. Ammazza is open late on weekends until midnight and there's a free lot next to the restaurant. $$

Babette's Café 573 North Highland Ave. Atlanta, Georgia 30307; (404) 523-9121   www.babettescafe.com

Steeped in history, this quaint restaurant, around for about two decades, is situated in a refurbished house built in 1916. With an outdoor deck that is prime real estate during warm months, it is a short cab ride away from downtown. Patrons especially like to visit during weekend for brunch as their French Toast with bananas and caramel sauce is outstanding. Don't miss the Babette's punch, a unique twist on a Mimosa. For dinner your best bet is to stick with the small plates. Order the Gaufrette potato with warmed gorgonzola cheese sauce and the mussels served with strawberries and Serrano peppers. Tuesday and Wednesday nights offer a 2 course prix fixe meal for $21. Babette's has a notable wine list. Reservations Recommended. $$$

Beetlecat 299 Elizabeth Street, Atlanta, GA 30307; (678) 732-0360 www.beetlecatatl.com

Named after the style of boat that was built in 1920 in the Northeast US, and another addition to the Ford Fry empire in the Inman Quarter district, is the nautical-themed, Beetlecat. Downstairs resembles a basement from the 70s and is first come seating. Upstairs is much more posh with reservations required. Most of the menu is small plates designed for sharing. Get the beef tartare with shrimp toast or the Cod or Snapper. $$$

Boccalupo 753 Edgewood Ave, Atlanta, GA 30307; (404) 577-2332 www.boccalupoatl.com

The fresh made pastas by Bruce Logue are delightful. The ambience definitely has a hipster feel. Logue's Black Spaghetti with Rock Shrimp which is his signature dish, is always on the menu. Killer cocktails are also available. The menu also has a couple "not noodle" dishes and some pleasing desserts. You can't tell it from the street view, but there's a lovely patio there as well. $$$

Bread and Butterfly 290 Elizabeth St, Atlanta, GA 30307; (678) 515-4536 www.bread-and-butterfly.com

Another restaurant in Inman Quarter, this French spot doesn't take reservations, so be prepared to wait. Looking for a Parisian bistro in the heart of the south? This is pretty close to it. It's got a lovely patio and large windows that open up for that perfect spring and fall weather. The ingredients are fresh and simple and the plates are small and a bit on the pricey side, but the ambiance is calming. Skip the limited dinner menu in favor of brunch where omelets shine here. Tip: Between 2:30 and 5:30 they offer many small plates for around $10. $$

Café Circa 464 Edgewood Avenue Atlanta, GA 30312; (404) 477-0008 www.cafecircaatl.com

Café Circa is one of the true hidden gems that border Edgewood and Boulevard. Their rooftop deck is inviting and looks like a fun time for a girls night out. The Caribbean menu has so many interesting sounding dishes on it. For starters choices include Jerk Wings, Curried Lamb Lollipops. For mains, you can't go wrong with the Cumin Dusted Salmon, Oxtail Osso Bucco or the Shrimp and Grits. Service is really friendly. $$$

DBA Barbecue – 1190 North Highland Avenue, Atlanta, GA 30306; (404) 249-5000 www.dbabarbecue.com

DBA or Doing Business As Barbecue is a long-favorite in Virginia Highland. Not your average barbecue joint, it's more upscale than you may expect. Plus, they cure their own ham and pastrami and smoke meats like duck and lamb in house too. It's complete with table service and incredible drinks and cocktail list. For a sampling of meats like ribs, brisket, turkey, chicken and more get the Whole House Platter which serves six for $75. Hosting a party? They do great catering as well. Owner Matt Coggin's iTunes playlist rocks too! $$

El Super Pan 675 Ponce De Leon Ave NE, Atlanta, GA 30308; (404) 477-0379 www.elsuperpan.com

 A creation of Chef Hector Santiago, it's located in the trendy Ponce City Market. The Melt in your mouth pork belly on a sweet coconut bun is delicious but don't discount the Smoked Tofu Bun. The Cuban or Media Dia topped with a chicharron is delightful, albeit pricey. Finish your meal with a Chocolate Chip Chipotle cookie, the spiciness enhancing the chocolate in the cookie. $$

Fontaine's Oyster House 1026 N Highland Ave Atlanta, GA 30306; (404) 872-0869 www.nightcapfoodandspirits.com/fontainesmainpage.html

Fontaine's was named after Fontaine Weyman, uncle of owner Sam Weyman. From the outside, the bright neon sign the marks Fontaine's is in stark contrast to the other Virginia Highland restaurants. Many patrons love the bar and sit and enjoy catching up with friends there or grabbing a meal alone. The bar spans the entire length of the restaurant and is a perfect option if you are flying solo. The Lobster bisque is excellent with large chunks of lobster and has the perfect combination of sweet and salty. Sides of tater tots and fried okra are highly recommended. They have complimentary valet. Tip: Tuesday nights feature a dozen oysters for $7. It is very popular and gets very crowded, so try to arrive early. $$

Folk Art 465 North Highland Avenue Northeast, Atlanta, GA 30307; (404) 537-4493 www.folkartrestaurant.com

A key tip to finding an awesome comfort food spot is when they serve breakfast all day, which Folk Art does. The kitschy design with old signs hanging on the brick walls gives the feeling of down home southern charm. One of the best items on the menu, however, is the gigantic Reuben. This is served with kimchi for a unique twist on a classic favorite. Also find pork chops and chicken and waffles on the menu. Don't miss out on the redneck cheese dip! $$

Fritti 311 N Highland Ave Atlanta, GA 30307; (404) 880-9559 www.frittirestaurant.com

Fritti pizza was one of the first Neapolitan pizzas around. Skip the appetizers and head for the main attraction: pizzas.

They have a ton of pizzas to choose from and there's a kind to suite anyone's taste. Although the standouts are the calamari pizza and the mushroom, if you are a meat lover order the Maialona, Fritti's version of a Meat Lover's. The soft, yet crispy crust is done just right. The smoked mozzarella is very fresh as are all the toppings. The wine list has many options by the glass. Be warned : it can get quite loud at this restaurant and tables are shoved very close together. Don't be fooled by the fact that it is a pizza joint - make reservations or expect to wait for a table.$$

Goin' Coastal 1021 Virginia Ave Atlanta, GA 30306; (404) 941-9117 www.goincoastalseafood.com

One of the first restaurants in the Atlanta to promote sustainable and farm-to-table and locally sourced foods was Goin' Coastal. Start your meal off with the fried pickles and their selection of fresh oysters that day. The presentation is beautiful. The wine list is great for those who enjoy wine, but don't miss out the imaginative and inventive cocktails that they offer. While there are obviously daily specials, the Trout lightly fried in Goin' Coastal's special seasoning blend is perfectly spiced. Meat lovers won't regret their choice either, as Pork Belly is tender and juicy too. $$$

Hampton + Hudson – 299 North Highland Avenue, Atlanta GA 30307; (404) 948-2123 www.hamptonandhudson.com

This cocktail bar / gastropub features leather tufted booths, and reclaimed wood all around the bar. The spot is good for diverse food preferences. Get items like Charred Octopus or a Wagyu Pastrami Sandwich. But don't miss out on the Low Country shrimp which is served in an exquisite sauce or the Beef Tartare tacos (in a potato chip shell). For a gastropub, there is a surprisingly generous amount of gluten free dishes and even a couple vegan items. It can get noisy on weekends, so visit on week nights for a more low key vibe. $$

Juliana's Crepes 775 Lake Avenue, Atlanta, GA 30307; (404) 436-1825 www.atlantacrepes.com

Hungarian crepes, called *palacsinta* are the specialty here. The menu features a mix of both sweet and savory crepes. For a savory crepe, get The Royal – made with Gruyere cheese, Tasso Ham and peach chutney. For a sweet crepe, you can't go wrong with the Cinnamon Baked Apple or the Pecan Pleasure. $

Kevin Rathbun Steak 154 Krog St #200, Atlanta, GA 30307; (404) 524-5600 www.kevinrathbunsteak.com

After making it big with his namesake restaurant, chef Rathbun decided to go bigger with a steakhouse. The two restaurants are located in close proximity to one another. And if you walk the Atlanta Beltline, you may catch him smoking a stogie out back. Start your meal with Yaya's Eggplant Fries or Pecan Fritters. A Roasted Bone Marrow is topped with Grand Marnier Jam. Dry-Aged Steak is the specialty and you can get it for up to 3 people. $$$$

Ladybird Grove & Mess Hall 684 John Wesley Dobbs Ave,
Atlanta, GA 30312; (404) 458-6838 www.ladybirdatlanta.
com

A hipster restaurant located along the Atlanta Beltline, it's
a great option to pop in for brunch when you are walking
the beltline. With categories like Trail Snacks, Campfire
and Basecamp (serves 3-4), the cuisine is best described as
playful Southern. The Chicken Fried Chicken is a good bet
with the S'mores for dessert. The bar gets crowded with
millennials looking to see and be seen weekends. Best bets
at brunch are the Nashville Hot Chicken Biscuit (biscuits are
made in house) and the Breakfast tacos made with Chorizo.
Add in a side of Roasted Grapefruit. $$

La Tavola 992 Virginia Ave, Atlanta, Georgia 30306; (404) 873-5430 www.latavolatrattoria.com

One of the staples of any neighborhood is a solid Italian restaurant, and La Tavola definitely fits the bill. The small dining room can get loud, especially given the open kitchen, so opt for patio dining open year round (they have heaters). The wine list is excellent and lengthy. Skip the pricey cocktails and go straight for wine. Start with the beet and orange salad. Dishes are highly creative like the pasta with Cuttlefish-Pancetta Ragu. Although dinners are phenomenal, don't overlook brunch. Try the Challah French Toast with berries and honey mascarpone. The perfectly done French toast marries perfectly with the sweet mascarpone and the tart berries. A house made polenta is a nice departure from the more traditional hash browns. Reservations necessary for weekend dining. Tip: Not feeling that hungry? Pasta entrees are available in appetizer portions for $5 less than the entree portion. $$$

Miso Izakaya 619 Edgewood Ave Atlanta, GA 30312; (678) 701-0128

An Izakaya is known as a place to sit, relax, drink and share small plates. Owner Guy Wong, has definitely created a pretty atmosphere for just that. Sochu, the Japanese version of vodka is used in many drinks mixed with items like Lychee, watermelon and cucumber. Start with the miso soup with crab. Then move on to the steamed buns, being sure to sample both the pork belly and duck which will perfectly whet your appetite for the star entrees to come. Sushi is fresh and well-prepared as are dishes like Tuna Tartar with quail egg on top, Madras Lamb and spicy Eggplant. Prices are low but add up quickly. $$$

Murphy's 997 Virginia Ave Atlanta, GA 30306; (404) 872-0904
www.murphys-atlanta-restaurant.com

One of the most popular brunch restaurants in the city, the wait can be hours long as diners line up outside in wait for some delicious breakfast favorites. Eggs and omelets are great but for a Southwestern fix give the Chilaquiles a try. At dinner the lights go down and dinner service turns cozy. Although the atmosphere is slightly upscale and classy, the food is one hundred percent comfort food. The spinach and sausage meatloaf is perfectly cooked. The shrimp and grits are consistently one of guests' favorite items on the menu. Skip the Truffled Mac n Cheese in favor of other sides. They also have a bakery and wine shop on site. $$$

One Eared Stag 1029 Edgewood Ave, Atlanta, GA 30307; (404) 525-4479 www.oneearedstag.com

You'll be greeted by animal heads hanging from the white brick walls at this uber hipster joint open for brunch, lunch and dinner. The menu, which changes frequently, best fits into the "New American" box. There's usually some sort of Rillettes on the menu, typically rabbit. Fish and seafood dishes trump meat ones here except for the burger, a la the "Meatstick" (two patties with Kraft cheese and a knife in the center). Tip: Don't want to drive? This spot is located in walking distance from the Inman Park MARTA Station. $$$

Original El Taco 1186 N Highland Ave Atlanta, GA 30306; (404) 873-4656 www.fifthgroup.com

Located away from the loud, busy bars, the crowd-pleasing Mexican restaurant and has a mix of young, middle-aged and families. When you enter the restaurant, you'll be given a numbered token. Every hour, they spin a huge wheel with prizes which range from the small chips and salsa to something much larger. Start things off with the "Just crushed" guacamole or the Queso Royale, which is has chorizo, charred onion and jalapenos for a bit of spice. Skips main entrees in favor of tacos. Most of the tacos are wonderful: chicken, fish, shrimp, carnitas, all offered with substantial meat inside. Tip: Can't make it to this location? They are located inside the Atlanta Airport too! $

Parish 240 N Highland Atlanta, GA 30307; (404) 681-4434 www.parishatl.com

Parish, a restaurant housed in a historic building from the early 1900s, with heavily influenced New Orleans style décor, has a southern menu, but pulls ethnic accents into each dish. Think okra with curry ketchup, sweet potato with Tahini, and barbecue carrots with Tzatziki sauce, The small menu is executed well. A grilled Rainbow Trout is paired with Kohlrabi and green tomato aioli. A Plenty of street parking is available or opt for valet. It's a great place for group dining. $$$

Rathbun's 112 Krog St R Atlanta, GA 30307; (404) 524-8280 www.rathbunsrestaurant.com

Rathbun's is as much about the food as it is about the famous chef, Kevin Rathbun. Staff is helpful and extremely knowledge about the menu, able to recommend a perfect wine pairing to compliment anything ordered. The menu is divided in to Small Plates, Big Plates and Second Mortgage Plates. Start with the Eggplant fries, huge and covered with powdered sugar. They are served with a side of Tabasco, the combination of sweet and spicy magnificent. Crispy Duck Breast with Risotto and Green Curry Essence is spicy, heat lovers will enjoy this filling dish. It can get rather loud in the restaurant. Note: The restaurant is closed on Sundays. $$$$

Serpas True Food 659 Auburn Ave. #501 Atlanta, GA 30312; 404-688-0040 www.serpasrestaurant.com

Starters here are small, so if you are famished, order three or four for a couple. Fried oysters and calamari, served with chili syrup are a tasty start to your meal. Some of the best entrees are the Airline Chicken and the Trout which is perfectly prepared. However, the Scallops in Panang curry sauce are one of the most popular menu items. The creamy grits are some of the best in the city. $$$

Sotto Sotto 313 North Highland Avenue Northeast, Atlanta, GA 30307; (404) 523-6678 www.urestaurants.com

There are two people who this restaurant is NOT for: those that have gluten intolerance and those that have an aversion to communal seating. Start with the Sea Scallops or the Prosciutto with Melon. There are four risottos on the menu and about a dozen pasta dishes. There's Gnocchi which they refer to as "Naked Ravioli", as well as a sweet sausage ragu named the "Priest Strangler" which are tasty. But a meat lover should get the Veal chop. $$$

Spice to Table 659 Auburn Ave NE #506, Atlanta, GA 30312; (404) 220-8945 www.spicetotable.com

When Asha Gomez shuttered her restaurant in Berkeley Heights, lots of diners were wondering what she would do next. Now open for lunch, this casual yet refined eatery delights with dishes like Kerala fried chicken. Large tables are perfect for group dining. There's lots of touches of Indian decor here. Don't miss out on the classic Chai done perfectly. Sometimes they have a special high tea you can take advantage of. $$

Staplehouse 541 Edgewood Ave SE, Atlanta, GA 30312; (404) 524-5005 www.staplehouse.com

Part of the Giving Kitchen, a non-profit that supports restaurant workers facing tragic circumstances, The Old 4th Ward restaurant received a James Beard Nomination for Best New Restaurant and was crowded *Bon Appetit* Magazine's Best Restaurant for 2016. The talent churns out some of the best food in the southeast and critics have taken note. Think items like duck with ramps and fava. Don't be surprised that a deposit of $85 per person is required for the five course tasting menu, only available Wednesday through Saturday. $$$$

Surin 810 N Highland Ave Atlanta, GA 30306; (404) 892-7789 www.surinofthailand.com

One of the first and most popular Thai restaurants in Atlanta, Surin remains quite popular. The seating is tight and it can get noisy on weekend nights when it is filled to capacity, so not a good option for a quiet evening. They have some of the best coconut soup in the city. For entrees the BBQ chicken at lunch is terrific. At dinner, don't miss out on the Snapper dishes. For soft-shell crab fans, get the flash fried soft shell crab with green curry sauce. Vegetarians will appreciate the tofu dishes (coconut soup and curry) both winners. Even such as basic dish the Pad Thai is spectacular here. Tip: Staff is quick to get you in and out at lunch. $$

The Sound Table 483 Edgewood Avenue Atlanta, GA 30312; (404) 835-2534 wwwthesoundtable.com

The Sound Table, located at the corner of Edgewood and Boulevard in Old 4th Ward area of Atlanta. It can be tricky to find as you'll need to look for the letters "S" and "T" written on the side of the wall, which identify the restaurant. The cocktail menu here is very elaborate, nearly more important than the food. Sample drinks include the *Stone Mountain* – made with Cognac, Pine liqueur, Pear liqueur, and baked apple bitters or the *September Gurl* – Made with Gemini Jams Fig Jam, Pisco, Lemon and Sage. For starters, order the Curried chickpeas and the Arancini (fried rice balls coated with breadcrumbs). The burger is quite tasty and juicy. Go ahead and splurge for the crispy, tasty fries too. $$

Taco Cowboy 1000 Virginia Ave Atlanta, GA 30306; (404) 815-9155 www.tomtomrestaurant.com

When Here to Serve restaurants abruptly closed their doors, many loyal customers were left bewildered about where they'd get this tap of unique tapas and seafood they were accustomed to at these restaurants. So, when Tom Catherall, a beloved Atlanta chef opened Taco Cowboy in the heart of the Virginia Highlands, his loyal customers came in droves to support him. Here you'll find deliciously presented items like steaks and bevy of tasty tacos. The chic restaurant Tip: The secret menu item (pictured above), Whole Fried Catfish, should not be missed.

Two Urban Licks 820 Ralph McGill Blvd, Atlanta, GA 30306; (404) 522-4622 www.twourbanlicks.com

Part of the Concentrics Restaurant Group, it's the best of the group and it's just plain sexy. No, your uber driver isn't taken you to a desolate area to violate you, it's just that the restaurant is located in a converted warehouse. You'll enter through what seems like an updated dock door and take a minute to take in the soaring fire pit. Once inside sexy, chic atmosphere creates a fun atmosphere whether celebrating with friends or there for a romantic evening. Servers are extremely knowledge about both the menu and the wine and make excellent wine / food pairings. Don't miss starting the meal off with one of the house made concoctions. The Smoked salmon with Chipotle cream cheese and Tuna tartare are not only a great start to the meal but a beautiful presentation. For entrees order the Skirt steak or Scallops and Grits. Tip: Secret late night menu is available after 10pm on weekends. $$$$

Venkman's 740 Ralph McGill Blvd, Atlanta, GA 30312; (470) 225-6162 www.venkmans.com

Care for a bit of entertainment with your meal? Then head to Venkman's where the music is as much the attraction as the food. A brunch menu is more exciting than dinner. Case in point, is their fabulous house made Bloody Mary. Entrees like Chicken and Grits or a special when available, Oxtail Chilaquiles are so filling you can skip the appetizer. Besides regular tables, there's a private dining room in the back, and a lovely patio or you can even sit at the bar. Note that a reservation doesn't guarantee the table for shows during a ticketed concert. You must purchase tickets separately. $$

Victory Sandwich 913 Bernina Ave., Atlanta, GA 30307; (770) 676-7287 www.vicsandwich.com

Sandwiches here are slider sized and slider priced. Try the Hambo: prosciutto, mozzarella, arugula apple, and reduced balsamic. Or try the The Castro - Slow-roasted pork, ham, fontina cheese, and yellow mustard. They even have a Pokémon, made with Korean BBQ, of course. You'll need to order two to get full. Or add a thoughtful side like ramen, cous cous or watermelon salad. It lends itself to the kind of establishment one would want to hang out, as they have a ping pong table and were also playing movies on the wall. The Jack-n-coke slushie is quite fabulous. They are open late, so it is a cool late night option. $

Wisteria 471 North Highland Ave. Atlanta, GA. 30307; 404-525-3363 www.wisteria-atlanta.com

Wisteria can be described as upscale Southern. Housed in a freestanding building with exposed brick and dark lighting it is extremely romantic, but also a fantastic choice to take an out of town guest. The wine list is huge – as thick as a book. Let your server pick one for you as they expertly pair wine with your food choices. The Black-Eyed Pea Hummus served up with home-made sweet potato chips had just the right amount of garlic and lemon juice. The scallops are another hit in the appetizer department. This is a twist on bacon-wrapped scallops using pork belly instead. Catfish, Shrimp and Grits and Fried Chicken are southern favorites on the menu, but there are more creative items like Pork and Dumplings, Icelandic Cod with Crab. $$$$

Zuma Sushi 701 Highland Ave Atlanta, GA 30312; (404) 522-2872 www.zumasushibar.com

The décor of Zuma Sushi is sleek and modern, using mostly red and black in their color palette. Although groups of friends frequent the establishment, it is mostly setup for couples. Note that it is a small staff that works here, so service, while friendly, can be slow at times. The Tuna Tataki is an excellent choice. Note that street parking can be difficult to find during peak times. There is a patio for outdoor seating when weather allows. $$

CHAPTER 5
Midtown

M idtown Atlanta is home to some of the finest restaurants in the city. While the heart of Midtown has been thriving for years now, there always seems to be events centered around bringing people to this neighborhood. The other big draw to Midtown is the arts. The High Museum of Art is located in Midtown as are other museums. Smaller playhouses are located here as well. So, it's the perfect place for a cultured date night.

5Church – 1197 Peachtree Street, Atlanta, GA 30361; (404) 400-3669 www.5church.com

Hailing from Charlotte, the restaurant has opened in one of the hottest pieces of real estate in Midtown. As you enter, the ceiling is painted with the words from the book, The Art of War and feathered light fixtures dangle above the bar. The sexy décor beckons you the settle in to the black leather booths and sip on a craft cocktail. But it's not all about appearances. 5Church delivers creative morsels like the Pastrami Cured Hamachi, Squid Ink Pasta, and ham and cheddar Agnolotti. But the crème de la crème is the Wagyu steak, priced at $15 per ounce. $$$

Antico Pizza 1093 Hemphill Ave Atlanta, GA 30318; (404) 873-1272 anticopizza.it

Antico sits in a small, non-descript building on the outskirts of Midtown proper. Touted as some of the best pizza in city, many of the ingredients used on the Neapolitan pizza are imported directly from Italy including the ovens. A unique feature of the "restaurant" is that they don't have a dining room but rather long wooden picnic tables that were brought into their kitchen for diners to eat as they never really intended to be a restaurant. Diners can sit at these communal tables and watch as their pizzas are made before their eyes, and served up piping hot after coming out of the 1000 degree oven. While the Margerita pizza is a customer favorite, don't miss out on the Diavaola (spicy peppers and soppressata) and the San Gennaro (sausage with sweet peppers). $$

Apache Café 64 3rd St Atlanta, GA 30308; (404) 876-5436 www.apachecafe.info

A breeding ground for raw talent, Apache Cafe holds a variety of artistic events including poetry readings, live shows, and art shows. Tip: There is also a back patio that will give you a breath of fresh air, should you need. It can get extremely packed with popular performances, so your best bet is to reserve online. NOTE: They do not accept credit cards at the door. The Jerk wings, Shrimp and Grits and quesadillas are the best bets. Save room for dessert – Sopapillas, Brown Sugared Plantains or Pear Cobbler. $$

Apres Diem 931 Monroe Dr E Ste C103 Atlanta, GA 30308; (404) 872-3333 www.apresdiem.com

Located in the Midtown Promenade center near to Piedmont Park, the restaurant is famous for coffee and desserts, but most Atlantans are unaware of the tasty and creative dinner items available. The dark and cozy atmosphere is reminiscent of cafes and bistros in Europe. The inviting couches and free Wi-Fi invite guest to hang out and drink coffee or something stronger. An added bonus is that there is free parking in the shopping center, a rarity in Midtown. Although they list Hummus and Baba Ghanouj separately on the menu, ask for combo, and servers are happy to accommodate. The most popular menu item, however, is the Salmon Farfalle, served in a Sambuca-Thyme cream sauce. Open late night: 2:00 Am on weekends and midnight all other nights. Come back for coffee and dessert after slipping next door to see a flick. Brunch features crab and lobster options at inexpensive prices. $$

Bacchanalia 1198 Howell Mill Rd Ste 100 Atlanta, GA 30318; (404) 365-0410 www.starprovisions.com

Bacchanalia is about an experience, not just exceptional food or service, of which both are just that, exceptional. The crowd tends to be an older one, mainly due to the hefty price tag that comes with dining here. Chefs and Owners Anne Quatrano and Clifford Harrison's culinary philosophy is to create light dishes built on strong flavors. The menu is seasonal, using organic and locally sourced items. By local, we mean sourced from Anne and Clifford's farm. For starters, get the Crab Fritter if it is available as it is nearly all lump crab. Menu items may include: Maple Leaf Duck, Red Snapper and Jamison Lamb. It is always rated one of Atlanta's top restaurants and the number one restaurant in the Zagat guide since 1996. Menu is a set four course prix fixe menu $85. The menu is composed of appetizer, entrée, cheese and dessert course. Closed on Sundays. $$$$

Baraonda 710 Peachtree St Atlanta, GA 30308; (404) 879-9962 www.baraondaatlanta.com

This rustic Italian spot serves everything from small, light dishes to hearty items like veal or rack of lamb. On the lighter side there's Octopus or the Gorgonzola salad. Pizza is

the star here served up on a thin, crispy crust. Try the Lamb Sausage Pizza or the Prosciutto di Parma Pizza. It is located in walking distance to The Fox Theatre, so lends itself to pre-theatre dining. However, note that the restaurant only accepts reservations for parties of 6 or more. They are open for both lunch and dinner. $$$

Better Half – 349 14th Street Building C, Atlanta GA 30318; (404) 695-4547 www.betterhalfatl.com

Blossoming from the popular supper club, Push Start Kitchen (the couple hosted sold out dinners in their hipster loft), each dish is a work of art, and blends the chef's time spent in Central America with his southern roots. Think Trout with black garlic Chilaquiles. The menu changes quite frequently, but one thing that never leaves is the Silk Handkerchief Pasta, what the chef made for his wife on their first date. The best deal is the five-course tasting menu for $55. Note: They are closed on Sundays and Mondays. $$$

Bocado 887 Howell Mill Road, Atlanta, GA 30318; (404) 815-1399 www.bocadoatlanta.com

I've told many a person to go here if they are seeking the burger in Atlanta. But their sandwiches are so glorious, it's hard to go wrong with any of them. And yes, go ahead and add those garlic fries to your order. Though the spot is a good option for a business lunch, they do a smaller menu at dinner that changes often, but is quite tasty. Think options like Flounder and Scallops. Tip: On Saturdays at dinner, they offer a delectable lobster roll available until sold out. $$

Bone Garden Cantina 1425 Ellsworth Industrial Blvd Ste 6 Atlanta, GA 30318; (404) 418-9072
www.bonegardencantina.com

Owned by the same owners as the Vortex, Bone Garden Cantina is a small restaurant tucked away in the West Midtown area. You certainly wouldn't stumble upon it, as it is located in an industrial area. As you enter the complex make sure you drive around back and this is where the entrance to Bone Garden is located. The space is rather small, but they took great care to decorate in the fashion of the Dia de los Muertos (Day of Dead), i.e. there are lots of skeletons painted on the wall. Start your meal off with an order of beet salad with oranges, and queso fresco topped with a vinaigrette dressing. Everything is a la carte here – tacos, enchiladas, burritos, making it possible to try many different things. Get the beef tongue (Lengua) or Pork Belly (Chicharron) tacos. For something heartier get the Mole Chicken Enchiladas. $$

Campagnolo 980 Piedmont Avenue, Atlanta, GA 30308; (404) 343-2446 www.campagnoloatl.com

If you like calamari and mussels you can certainly start with those, but the Arancini (baked risotto with balsamic reduction and fried) is better. So is the Cannellini Bruschetta. Simple pasta dishes like Gnocchi with Arugula pesto or the Lasagna with béchamel steal the show but pricey dishes like lamb or steak don't disappoint either. Tip: The patio is dog friendly, so bring your fur kids. $$$

Carolyn's Gourmet 1151 W Peachtree St Atlanta, GA 30309; (404) 607-8100   www.carolynsgourmetcafe.com

There is a great ambiance with the exposed brick walls. Sandwich have quirky names like Motivation (hot turkey and Swiss with cole slaw and thousand island dressing on pumpernickel) to Commitment to Excellence (a BLT with blue cheese), or the High-energy - delicious tuna melt with just a tad of mayo. You can also find quesadillas, burgers, salads, pizzas and wraps. It isn't only the food that impressive. The service is also something to brag about. The staff is friendly and the food comes out quickly. Tip: If you are a South Carolina Gamecock this is the spot for you to get your game on. $

Cooks & Soldiers 691 14th St NW, Atlanta, GA 30318; (404) 996-2623 www.cooksandsoldiers.com

With restaurants like Iberian Pig and Double Zero successfully under their belts, the restaurant group behind this Spanish tapas restaurant, focusing on the Basque region, certainly knows what it is doing. The menu consists of small snacks, or Pintxos, and well as grilled meats. One of the most interesting is the tomato tartare with a carrot yolk in the center. Get the grilled Octopus and a variety of toasts topped with items like figs or mushrooms or anchovies. A perfectly prepared steak is flawless, but pork tenderloin is excellent as well. $$$

Cypress Street Pint and Plate 817 W Peachtree St Ste E125
Atlanta, GA 30308; (404) 815-9243 www.cypressbar.com

Cypress Street was a welcome addition to the Midtown
neighborhood, providing, a bar within walking distance to
the many condos and apartments in the area. There are
dark woods around the bar and booths, and surprisingly the
crowd doesn't seem to all be the young twenty-somethings
that patronize the nearby bars. Perhaps it is because Cypress
Street has a much more sophisticated beer menu than
neighboring restaurants. The patio is fantastic – a large brick
area that has fire pits in the winter and is a fun place to hang

on warm summer evenings. The food is typical bar food – sandwiches, pizza, wings and the like. One unique menu item is the Sublime Burger (see above) – the burger buns are made of a Sublime Doughnut and said burger is topped with bacon, caramelized onions, and cheddar cheese. $$

Ecco 40 7th St NE Atlanta, GA 30308; 404-347-9555 www.ecco-atlanta.com

Located in the heart of Midtown, Ecco is Mediterranean food with an excellent wine list and cocktails. There is a nice complexity of flavors to everything on the menu. To start, you're missing out if you don't get the Fried Goat Cheese. Drizzled with honey it is amazing. Don't be fooled by the small portions in the appetizers, they are very filling. For entrees you can't go wrong with the fish as they are all executed perfectly. Pastas taste like they are house made and the wood-fired pizzas are creative and come with quality toppings. Think sausage, grana padano and house made mozzarella. You'll want to save room for dessert with items like Cardamom Rice Pudding. Note: There is also a location in the Atlanta airport. $$$

Eight Sushi Lounge 999 Brady Avenue, Atlanta, GA 30318;
(404) 796-8888 www.eightsushiatl.com

Don't be fooled by the name. The space is not part restaurant, part bar, they take food seriously at this sophisticated Westside spot. Start you evening off with the Damson in Disguise, Eight's twist on a classic margarita. With a mix of cooked items and sushi, there's something for everyone, making this a superb choice for groups. Start with the Moshi Moshi Oysters or Snapper Carpaccio. You can even call ahead and have them arrange an Omakase (chef's special menu) for you. Signature rolls are noticeably absent of the creamy sauces prevalent at other spots, letting the quality of fish come through. A Nigiri platter features a buttery Escolar. $$$

Empire State South 999 Peachtree St Atlanta, GA 30309; (404) 541-1105 www.empirestatesouth.com

Chef / Owner Hugh Acheson wow guests with his restaurant that focuses on locally-sourced Southern cuisine. The inventive menu pairs new and different ingredients with old favorites like the Kimchi Rice Grits. While the dinner service is solid, the restaurant does its best at lunch. The Trout with bacon vinaigrette is probably one of the best dishes on the menu. There's also a dish called the Super Food, which offers a sampling of five different items: Hanger Steak, a small salad and various in-season vegetables. The restaurant will make you love your vegetables even if you've never been one to enjoy them. Empire State South serves breakfast, lunch and dinner Monday through Friday and serves Brunch and Dinner on weekends. Want to get your bocce ball on? They also have a Bocce Ball court too. Tip: They validate parking for three hours in the nearby parking garage. $$$$

Flip Burger 1587 Howell Mill Rd, Atlanta, GA 30318; (404) 343-1609 www.flipburgerboutique.com

Brought to you by Top Chef, Richard Blais, Flip Burger is an upscale burger spot. Think white leather seating and over the top picture frames surrounding flat screen TVs. There are a bevy of both classic and twists on burgers like the Chorizo or Oaxaca burgers. Oh you're vegetarian? No problem. Get the Fauxlafel burger made of chickpeas. Of course, there's also the nitro milkshakes with flavors like the Krispy Kreme or Nutella and Burnt Marshmallow. There's another location in Buckhead, but the original is still the best. Tip: They have pop up specials like a lobster dinner for $20. $$$

Ginya Izakaya – 1700 Northside Drive, #A5, Atlanta, GA 30318; (470) 355-5621 www.ginyaatlanta.com

There are many who love Japanese food and are thrilled to have an Izakaya that is closer to the north side of town. Tonkatsu Ramen dish is fantastic. Expect to find many sushi options as well. Prices are inexpensive, but the décor is upscale. It's a good choice if you are short on time as the food comes out quickly. Note they are only open for dinner. $$

Gio's Chicken 1099 Hemphill Ave NW, Atlanta, GA 30318; (404) 347-3874 www.littleitalia.com

By the same folks as Antico Pizza (an incredibly popular Neapolitan pizza spot) Gio's is a fast casual spot offering...you guessed it...chicken dishes. The Sorrento Lemon Chicken as well as the Scarpiello are must haves. But if you like it spicy get the Diavolo. Save some dough when you BYOB. Tip: You can order pizza from Antico to go and take that home after chowing down here. They are closed on Mondays. $$

GRAIN Bar – 856 W Peachtree, Atlanta, GA 30308; (404) 881-5377 www.grain-bar.com

Don't blink or you might miss GRAIN in Midtown. The small bar features a selection of sharable plates but the highlight is the oysters. And happy hour is 4-6 pm Monday through Friday and features $1 oysters. A selection of cheese and charcuterie is the perfect way to follow up the oysters. Make sure to get the Mortadella Mousse and Speck. There's a terrific selection of location beers, but the bartenders are adept at making a cocktail that delights if you just give them an idea of your favorite flavors. Open late until 3 am on weekends. $$

Hankook Taqueria 1341 Collier Road Atlanta, GA 30318; (404) 352-8881 www.hankooktaqueria.com

Grabbing a hold of the Korean Taco craze, Hankook garnered quite the following since opening. There's no table service at Hankook. Order at the counter, and stick that number on your table and staff delivers food quickly. The staff is extremely friendly and the lack of table service helps to keep prices low. The smallish restaurant, located in the industrialized area on the Westside, can get very busy when the lunch crowd descends, so try to visit at off peak times as parking is limited. Menu choices are tacos, burritos (standard chicken, beef, pork, fish, tofu, shrimp) and what they like to call "Street Snacks" (sides) like fried sweet potatoes and dumplings. Quite often the "special" of the day is the Calamari taco, one of the best tacos there and not to be missed. $

JCT Kitchen 1198 Howell Mill Rd #18, Atlanta, GA 30318; (404) 355-2252 www.jctkitchen.com

Under the direction of Ford Fry, JCT Kitchen turns out some incredible tasty dishes with a slightly Southern spin. The Angry Mussels, cooked up with bacon, were once featured on The Food Network, so it remains a "must-try" for many who visit the restaurant. One of the most popular dishes on the menu is Fried Chicken. Trout is another standout dish. There's also a lovely rooftop patio that is fun for socializing and even has live music on certain nights. Tip: Since the parking lot serves for many other restaurants, it gets full fast. However, there is ample free parking to be found in the parking deck located across the bridge from the restaurant and it is a short and pleasant walk. $$$

Livingston 659 Peachtree St Atlanta, GA 30308; (404) 897-5000 www.livingstonatlanta.com

Livingston is an ultra-chic and well-appointed restaurant and bar located across the street from the famous Fox Theatre. The design is history meets modern and trendy. Start your meal off with the trout spread. Get the delicious Shrimp and Grits if you want southern food, but the Scallops are a customer favorite, with Tasso and corn chowder. Tip:

The offer a brunch buffet for Saturday and Sundays before shows at the Fox Theatre. Don't forget to get your parking validated. $$$$

Lure 1106 Crescent Avenue, Atlanta, GA 30309; (404) 817-3650 www.lure-atlanta.com

Part of the Fifth Group restaurant group, this seafood restaurant is located in the center of Midtown. Try the bottle shop cocktails while you are enjoying some of the oysters at this Midtown spot. Plus don't miss out on the Tuna Poke served with shrimp chips. Scallops are a highlight, too. Vegetarians will enjoy a Cauliflower Steak. $$$

Mary Mac's Tea Room 224 Ponce de Leon Ave Atlanta, GA 30308; (404) 876-1800 www.marymacs.com

Mary Mac's is one of the truly iconic restaurants that have graced Atlanta for 70 years. Back in the 1940s, there were 16 tea rooms in Atlanta. Although not a place that served tea, these were a fancied up versions of a meat and three. They were centers for neighborhoods where families and friends could spend an afternoon. Today, Mary Mac's is the only tea room that remains in Atlanta. Famous celebrities like Richard Gere, Beyoncé and Paula Deen have diner here. Although a signature drink is the Peach Martini, don't visit without sampling their sweet tea, featured in Travel and Leisure Magazine. Everything on the menu is quite tasty like fried okra, salmon cakes, fried green tomatoes, fried chicken tenders, fried crawfish and ribs. Tip: All first time guests are treated to a sample Pot Likker (go and find out what it is!) $$

Miller Union 999 Brady Ave Atlanta, GA 30318; (678) 733-8550 www.millerunion.com

The restaurant occupies the old space of the Miller Union Stockyards, hence the name. The menu focuses on farm-to-table dining, however some of the more popular items seem to never leave the menu. When settling in, order the Miller Thyme (gin, lemonade and thyme). The drinks are well-crafted here and use high end liquor. Charcuterie plates don't disappoint with options like Pastrami Beef Tongue, Duck Prosciutto, Duck Liver Terrine, they are unique a definitely a good fit for foodies. Another exceptional starter is the farm egg baked in celery cream with grilled bread. Skip seafood in favor of duck, rabbit or pork dishes. $$$$

Nan Thai Fine Dining 1350 Spring St Atlanta, GA 30309; (404) 870-9933 www.nanfinedining.com

The ambience of Nan is unforgettable. From the giant golden tamarind outside to the rattan-style furniture inside, to the servers wearing traditional attire, attention to detail is evident. Everything relating to design and aesthetics is well-planned and is very eye-catching. The interior also features an open kitchen displaying herbs and spices. It is truly beautiful. Nan is the sister restaurant to long time Thai favorite Tamarind, also located in Midtown. Get the Lamb Shank, with Thai red curry. Love seafood? Get the Panang Talay, made with prawns, scallops and calamari. $$$$

ONE Midtown Kitchen 559 Dutch Valley Rd Atlanta, GA 30324 (404)-892-4111 www.onemidtownkitchen.com

Part of the Concentrics Restaurant Empire, the allure of the neon sign, it's swanky bar scene and modern look, still make One Midtown Kitchen a pretty hot Atlanta destination. But even years later, they don't rest on their laurels, giving both the décor and menu an update when necessary. The bar scene is a destination all by itself, with its wall of wines and specialty cocktails, it can make for a fun couples evening or girls night out. Start with the Calamari or Pork Belly. Any fish dishes are exceptional, and steak lovers will enjoy the Steak Frites. Desserts are small but decadent, so don't overlook them! $$$

Park 75 75 14th St Atlanta, GA 30309; (404) 253 3840
www.fourseasons.com/atlanta/dining/park_75

As one would expect with the Four Seasons (where Park 75 is located), the caliber of this restaurant is top notch. Stepping inside, one immediately gets the feeling of regality that the Four Seasons exudes. However, it isn't stuffy. Service is pleasant and attentive. The kitchen can address special diets like gluten intolerance very easily. There's a nod to Southern cuisine with starters like Pork Belly and mains of Shrimp and Grits and Georgia Trout. The seafood like Tuna Tartare, oysters, crab and more is extremely fresh. At brunch, the coffee is brewed just right. However, make sure to start brunch off with a Bloody Mary as Four Seasons serves up their rather large one in a large mason jar. $$$$

Pasta da Pulcinella 1123 Peachtree Walk Atlanta, GA 30309; (404) 876-1114 pastadapulcinella.com

Located in a converted house as many of the restaurants that line the side streets of Midtown, the house is charming and quaint and heavy on romance. The view of the nearby skyscrapers is impressive. It is a perfect place to celebrate a birthday or anniversary with that special someone. The bar mixes up fantastic cocktails, however, the wine list is quite large and worth sampling a couple glasses. There are several vegetarian entrees on the menu, so a good choice or those who don't eat meat. The Ravioli Sardi Di Melanzane is a vegetarian entrée meat lovers will love. With eggplant, bell peppers, walnuts, ricotta, parmigiano, basil, and mint it packs in a lot a flavor. Probably the most popular item is the Tortelli di Mele, ravioli filled with browned Granny Smith apples, sausage, and parmigiano. The combination of sweet apples and salty sausage is a winning taste. The house is relatively small, so reservations are a must, especially on weekends. $$$

Pig and the Pearl 1380 Atlantic Ave Ste 14180 Atlanta, GA 30363; (404) 541-0930 www.thepigandthepearl.com

Can't decide between seafood or barbecue? You're covered at Atlantic Station's Pig and the Pearl. Dinner is much better than lunch and works well for groups...if you like sharing. Order one of the reasonably priced punches to start. A seafood tower with oysters, shrimp and tuna tartare is outstanding. Indulge in the Pimento Cheese Fritters as well. Skip ribs in favor of the meaty brisket and you won't be disappointed. Tip: Oysters are just a buck every day from 4-6 pm. $$

Pijiu Belly 678 10th St Atlanta, GA 30318; (404) 343-6828
www.pijiubelly.com

The word, "Pijiu" is Mandarin for "beer". So you can imagine that they have a pretty decent craft beer list, but the cocktail list is impressive as well. The concepts is comfort food with Asian influence. Think items like Thai Tater Tots or a Bulgogi Cheesesteak. Don't miss the Grit Stix, topped with glutton-ous bacon. There is rotisserie chicken for those looking to eat a bit healthier. They are open for brunch with items like chicken and waffles, a much likely with far shorter waits than other Midtown spots. $$

Proof and Provision 659 Peachtree St Atlanta, GA 30308; (404) 597-5045 www.proofandprovision.com

You wouldn't expect a glamorous hotel to have a reason-able priced speakeasy but it does. Once inside the Georgian Terrace hotel, head down to the basement. This is a terrific option if you are seeing a show at the Fox Theatre, located directly across the street. Tasty cocktails and comfort food await you in this basement bar. Simple items like duck wings and grilled cheese are some of my favorite dishes here. $$

Rreal Tacos 100 6th St NE #110, Atlanta, GA 30308; (404) 458-5887 www.rrealtacos.com

Rreal Tacos marries Chef Adrian Villarreal's training in Le Cordon Bleu Paris with his Mexican heritage. The modern and industrial look is augmented with bright colors to add a touch of warmth. They've even incorporated Talavera tiles, imported from Puebla, Mexico. Skip booze for house made drinks like Tamarind and Horchata. Pay the small upgrade for the house made corn tortillas. Get the Pork Trompo which is spinning on a vertical skewer when you enter the restaurant.

They have lunch specials and it is one of the better for you options in the area. $

Restaurant Eugene 2277 Peachtree Rd Atlanta, GA 30309; (404) 355-0321 www.restauranteugene.com

This is definitely a splurge worthy restaurant. Think birthdays and anniversaries. The staff here takes special care to make sure you and your guest are well taken care of. Chef Hopkins has embraced the farm to table movement and as such, you can expect to find locally sourced items on the menu. When ordering, menu items can be ordered a la carte or you can order from the chef's 5-course tasting menu. There's also a wine pairing available if you really want to splurge. Don't miss the pork belly appetizer. The flavors are delicate and delicious at the same time, with the shallots and sorghum marrying well with the creamy greens. Another star appetizer is the Trout or Tuna Tartare. Salmon and Duck entrees are incredible here. Reservations are a must. $$$$

Saltwood 1065 Peachtree Street, Atlanta, GA 30309; (470) 239-1962 www.saltwoodatlanta.com

Located inside the Loews Hotel, Saltwood differs from your average hotel restaurant in several ways. For cocktails, a Saltwood Dog, with gin, pink grapefruit and honey struck the right balance of tart and sweetness. Kudos to Saltwood for not sticking it to guests with low quality, overpriced cocktails like many hotels do. With locally sourced items, they keep prices low. The menu is much edgier than you'd find at hotel restaurants as well. Offal like beef tongue and Veal Sweetbreads, fried with an almond crust, and served with scallion and mint jam, are definitely winning dishes. If there are any shortcomings it is a slightly inexperienced staff. $$$

Sausalito West Coast 1422 West Peachtree St Atlanta, GA 30309; (404) 532-0032 www.sausalitowestcoast.com

This Mexican restaurant is only open Monday through Friday for lunch 11 – 4pm. Nearby office workers know that this place has great food and it gets very crowded at peak times. Although it is not overly fancy, they do have quality food. Their steak tacos are highly recommended. The lightly seasoned steak is cut when orders for tacos or burritos are placed, not pre-sliced like a fast food joint. Don't do beef? Order the sunset tacos with Mahi Mahi. Salads come with a unique Blackberry Habanero dressing giving it a nice kick. Tip: Only a short walk from the High Museum or Colony Square area. $

Silver Skillet 200 14th St Atlanta, GA 30318; (404) 874-1388 www.thesilverskillet.com

An Atlanta institution, it has been around for over 55 years. Silver Skillet is another Atlanta restaurant that was featured on the Food Network. *Diners, Drive-Ins and Dives* host Guy Fieri stopped in to check it out. For those wanting to experience a Southern breakfast in an Atlanta landmark, then they need look no further. The biscuits and grits (a staple in any good Southern breakfast) are quite spectacular here. Try the Pork Chop breakfast as it is a favorite of many Atlantans. Servers are friendly, the place has a cozy, nostalgic feel about it and plays hits from the 50s and 60s for a real diner feel. Note: It is not open late. In fact, the restaurant closes around 2 pm. so don't plan on visiting for dinner. $

South City Kitchen 1144 Crescent Ave, Atlanta, GA 30309; (404) 873-7358 www.southcitykitchen.com

Planning a night on the town in Midtown? SCK has the atmosphere to kick off your festivities. Though they've expanded to several locations, the original is the most fun. The southern cuisine is upscale yet not fussy. Pimento cheese is served with house made pickles and Fried Green Tomatoes are served with a red pepper coulis. Georgia Trout is paired with heirloom carrots and bok choy. A standout is the Shrimp and Grits, which has Tasso ham and lovely poblano peppers. Get a table upstairs overlooking all the action in the kitchen below. $$$

STK Atlanta 1075 Peachtree St, Atlanta, GA 30309; (404) 793-0144 togrp.com/restaurant/stk-atlanta

STK is the epitome of sexiness when it comes to Atlanta restaurants. The swanky atmosphere is perfect for a romantic birthday dinner. Sip on a colorful cocktail as you nuzzle up to your sweetie in the comfy booths. Indulge in a lamb shoulder starter or beef tartare. For entrees, scallops don't disappoint, but at least one person must get a steak. I recommend the Sirloin, dripping with butter and served with eight, *yes eight* dipping sauces. $$$$

Sublime Doughnuts 535 10th St NW Atlanta, GA 30318; (404) 897-1801 www.sublimedoughnuts.com

Some would argue are some of the best doughnuts in Atlanta. Sublime Doughnuts was started by Atlanta resident, Kamal Grant. After studying at the Culinary Institute of America in New York, Grant soon found his calling to be making pastries. In fact, the Sublime Doughnuts Grant churns out are so delicious and complex in flavor, they are more like pastries than any doughnut you've ever eaten. Everyone that visits has their own favorite. $

Tabla 77 12th St NE #2, Atlanta, GA 30309; (404) 464-8571 www.tablaatlanta.com

Tabla is a type of Indian drum that dates back to the 13th century. Rather than being played with sticks, the musician uses their hands and the instrument allows for more complicated rhythm structures than with typical drums. In Atlanta, Tabla should be synonymous with modern Indian served in a posh atmosphere. Drinks are creative here as well. A Chai Old Fashioned is made with Chai infused Whiskey, and their signature Tabla Margarita, made with tamarind paste. Surprisingly, their mocktails are just as impressive, if not more than the cocktails. Traditional Indian dishes can be found on the menu as well a lamb shank that is a must try. The huge shank was served with fragrant and colorful rice, but who can resist adding an order of naan as well? The Roomali Roti is made with half wheat and half flour and totally delicious. $$$

Tamarind 1197 Peachtree St Ste Atlanta, GA 30361; (404) 873-4888 www.tamarindseed.com

Tamarind is the less expensive version of its sister restaurant Nan Thai Fine Dining. For appetizers, skip the more common rolls, and splurge for the Green Papaya salad. The ever popular, Pad Thai, is perfectly done here (not overly sweet). Stand out dishes are the Green Curry and Kai-Pad-Prik-Kingh. For a beautiful presentation order the Siam Chicken, which comes served in half of a pineapple. The restaurant has various pepper levels to choose from, so start with level two and work your way up. Get a Thai Iced tea or coffee during or after your meal, for a refreshing, slightly sweet pick me up. Especially if staying at the W Hotel in Midtown, this restaurant a much better alternative than the main hotel restaurant. $$$

TAP: A Gastropub 1180 Peachtree Street, Atlanta, GA 30309; (404) 347-2220 www.tapat1180.com

Although a fabulous dinner awaits at this gastropub (many with ethnic influences), brunch is a lovely options that many ignore here. Buck trend of a Bloody Mary, in favor of non-traditional cocktails, like The Cherokee Rose, a refreshing cocktail, made with guava puree. A delightful scotch pepper comes with a violet colored sauce. The Southern Benedict is sure to please anyone wanting a filling brunch. Two fried chicken pieces sit on top of a biscuit, along with pimento cheese, eggs. At dinner, burgers, fish and tacos are terrific $$$

Tapa Tapa 931 Monroe Dr, Atlanta, GA 30308; (404) 481-5226
www.tapatapaatlanta.com

Located in the same center as their sister restaurant, Apres Diem, this dimly lit restaurant features classic tapas you're familiar with and even a delicious Paella. Other interesting tapas include Salmon Carpaccio with Trout Roe plus Brussels Sprouts with a Roasted Red Pepper Glaze. There's a monthly wine and tapas pairing. There's live Latin music on Friday evenings. Wednesdays and Thursdays are half off bottles of wine. $$$

Tavernpointe 1545 Peachtree St NE #101, Atlanta, GA 30309; (404) 549-3954 www.tavernpointe.com

Besides many local beers on draft and a terrific selection of wines, all wines are offered by the glass or bottle. The Time Invested cocktail with tequila, pear cordial, green tea and celery bitters is balanced perfectly, not too strong or sweet. Dining solo? You won't feel lonely at the convivial bar grazing on selections from the Snacks or Appetizers section of the menu. With a group, get the Mussels our Poutine Fries. The Mussels are fantastic with the saffron and smoky tomatoes. For entrees get Swordfish or try their Smoked Peruvian Meats. Their smoked meats are sure to have you coming back with their slow roasted flavor and juicy morsels. Make sure you save room to at least share one dessert as Tavernpointe's chef makes the desserts in house, like the sticky toffee date cake. $$$

Taqueria del Sol 1200 Howell Mill Rd NW Atlanta, GA 30318; (404) 352-5811 www.taqueriadelsol.com

Nominated for a James Beard award in the "Outstanding Restauranteur" category, there's a reason crowds keep coming back to Taqueria del Sol. The restaurant is able to mix in authentic Mexican flavors into their food but still have wide appeal. In addition, since the items are a la carte prices are kept extremely low. Don't be deterred by the long lines that form outside the restaurant, they move quickly as food comes out quickly. House rules are not to grab a table until your food is ready as tables turn over in a hurry. Start with the amazing cheese dip and Shrimp and Corn chowder. Order the fish or fried chicken tacos lime-jalapeño mayonnaise. Margaritas are excelled and prepared with the perfect mix of tequila and sweet stuff, so don't miss out on trying one. $

West Egg Café 1100 Howell Mill Rd NW Atlanta, GA 30318; (404) 872-3973 www. westeggcafe.com

Known for their phenomenal cupcakes, most visitors can't resist picking at least one up on their way out. With flavors like Red velvet, and Hummingbird, they deliver a lot of flavor in a small portion. While the menu has many breakfast and brunch favorites, there is a decidedly Southern slant to their options. Items like Hummus and Collard Greens and Fried Green tomatoes are prominent on the menu. Open for breakfast lunch, they do serve breakfast all day long. For lunch get the Cuban or PB&J Burger. Brunch favorites include the Challah French Toast or the Chilaquiles. They offer free Wi-Fi and there's plenty of free parking is available in the deck behind the restaurant. $$

Woody's Cheesesteaks 981 Monroe Dr NE Atlanta, GA 30308; (404) 876-1939 No website

The tiny operation cranks out some extremely tasty Cheesesteaks in this side of the Mason Dixon line. True Philadelphians might say it is not completely authentic. But this rather tiny little hut has quite a following, so be prepared to wait a while for you sandwich. Don't expect to be in and out in a couple minutes, since everything is cooked to order. Of course they offer other sandwiches and hot dogs, but the star of the show here are the Cheesesteaks. Get the "All the Way" with onions, ketchup or load it up with mushroom and banana peppers. Either way, you won't regret it. The parking lot is small, but when available, there's a quaint little outdoor eating area. $

Urban Cannibals Bodega + Bites 368 5th St NE, Atlanta, GA 30308; (404) 230-9865 No website

Urban Cannibals is part grocery store, part deli, and part restaurant all in one. Not only do they have meats, vegetables and other staples to cook with at home, but while you're shopping you can place an order to go. So, this is great spot to pick up something to take home too. Highly recommend the Reuben (regular or Turkey), The Cuban sandwich or the Lamb gyro. It is a good spot for vegetarians too. They even make a tofu gyro. They serve brunch and dinner in addition to lunch options. Call ahead as wait times can be long during peak hours. $

CHAPTER 6
Decatur, Emory and Druid Hills

The city of Decatur has seen quite a transformation in the last decade, with much kudos from magazines near and far. Award-winning restaurants have chosen to locate here as well. What Decatur residents love about it is that it has the small town feel, but it is extremely close to all the amenities the city has to offer. Even those that don't live in Decatur, drive from pretty far (yes, me) to experience this friendly, easy-going, yet hip city. Don't have a car? No problem. MARTA Decatur station goes right into the Decatur square.

57th Fighter Group Restaurant 3829 Clairmont Rd Atlanta, GA 30341; (770) 234-0057 www.the57threstaurant.com

The 57th Fighter Group Restaurant has been an Atlanta institution since opening some twenty years ago. With its WWII theme, The main dining area of the restaurant has great views of the small Dekalb-Peachtree airport runways. The menu features American classics. Menu highlights are the Pork Chop and Stuffed Trout with shrimp and avocado cream. Steaks and burgers are also available. There are private rooms and a patio area great for groups. Smaller tables lend themselves to more intimate dining but still allow views of runways. A fantastic brunch is available on Sundays. Closed Mondays $$$

Brick Store Pub 125 E Ct Sq Decatur, GA 30030; (404) 687-0990 www.brickstorepub.com

Located in the heart of Decatur, it is hard to miss the Brick Store Pub. The décor is brick walls and a wood bar, tables and stools. Of the two levels of the pub, the bottom tends to be much more open and less crowded, while the top is where most like to congregate. Extremely popular, expect a full house no matter what night of the week it is. The extensive beer list has a heavy focus on Belgian beers. The menu isn't large but what they make, they do quite well. Skip burgers in favor of sandwiches, especially the Chicken Salad Melt, made with dates, pine nuts and cream cheese, served on wheat berry bread. For entrees the house special Fish & Chips is served hot and crispy and lives up to its reputation. $$

Brush Sushi Izakaya 316 Church St Decatur, GA 30030; (678) 949-9412 www.brushatl.com

Named after the fact that each piece of sushi is brushed with house made soy sauce, this spot has filled a void for Japanese in Decatur. You'll find offal here like chicken hearts and pork belly, but there's sushi and yakitori as well. Nigiri is tasty but very pricey as is the Omakase dinner. Skip sushi and order small cooked plates off the menu and enjoy a tapas style dinner. Get the pork belly, Wagyu and Uni dishes. If you have room for dessert get the Matcha cake, served in a cast iron skillet. If you like Sake, they have a good selection and even have it on tap. If you like ramen, they have it late evenings (after 9pm) Tuesdays through Thursdays. Closed on Mondays. $$$

Café Alsace 121 E Ponce De Leon Ave Decatur, GA; 30030 (404) 373-5622   www.cafealsace.net

This tiny French restaurant located near the Decatur Square is easy to miss, so be on the lookout. The quaint and cozy little restaurant doesn't fit many dinners, probably only thirty at the most. But it does have loyal customers. There are eclectic French novelties on display and even for sale. One of the most popular menu items is the Pate, which they sell by the pound, for those who want to take some home. Another staple on the menu is the Coq au Vin. Flavorful and aromatic, this dish is not to be missed. French classics like Chicken Cordon Bleu and Beef Bourguignon are on the menu as well. The French staff is cheerful and friendly. Brunch is quite affordable too. Closed Mondays. $$$

Cakes and Ale 155 Sycamore Street, Decatur, GA 30030; (404) 377-7994 www.cakesandalerestaurant.com

The name comes from a Shakespeare term, which means "All good things in life." Despite the name, the restaurant is not big on cakes or ale. The upscale menu changes often, depending on what is available locally. You'll find about half a dozen appetizers and the same amount of entrees on the menu. Get the Arancini or fresh fish. Be warned: portions are small and you'll spend a small fortune here. Service can be hit or miss. The restaurant isn't huge and is quite popular on weekends, so be sure to make reservations (credit card required) well in advance. $$$$

Café Lily 308 W Ponce De Leon Ave Ste B Decatur, GA 30030; (404) 371-9119 www.cafelily.com

This Decatur neighborhood restaurant borrows its cuisine from many countries around the Mediterranean including: Italy, France, Greece, Spain, North Africa, and the Middle East. The menu has everything from Italian style Eggplant, to Spanish Tortas with Chorizo, to Souvlaki. At lunch try the "PLP" which is a twist on the BLT, made with Pancetta. At dinner an appetizer of Pan de Higo or Fig cake with Manchego cheese, Serrano ham is a nice start. For entrees try the Pinchitos, Spanish lamb served with Picante salsa verde. It also boats a Wine Spectator Award for its comprehensive wine offering. $$$

Calle Latina 406 Church Street, Decatur, Georgia 30030; (404) 378-0020 callelatinaatlanta.com

The small space is bursting with personality. You must start with some empanadas as they make some of the best in Atlanta. The black bean with goat cheese as well as the chicken with mole. For entrees get the pork slab, served with cilantro rice or the Mahi Mahi. For traditional dessert, go with the Tres Leches Cake or for something non-traditional get the Passion Mousse Cake topped with ginger orange couli. $$

Chai Pani – 406 W. Ponce de Leon Ave Decatur, GA 30030; (404) 378-4030 www.chaipanidecatur.com

A bright mural greets you as you enter Chai Pani. Fragrant and lively, this is Indian street food at its best. They make Indian food very approachable, especially for those who (think) they don't like it. Think items like Kale Pakoras and Okra Fries. Get the Sloppy Jai, a Spiced lamb hash or the Bengali Fish Fry made with Catfish. And don't overlook the creative cocktails that they have. The Sharaabi Nimbu with Meyer Lemon Vodka, triple sec, pineapple, lime, and vanilla was outstanding. They also have bottled cocktails too. Not drinking? The Lime Rickey and the Nimbu Pani are spectacular mocktails. $

Community Q 1361 Clairmont Rd North Decatur, GA 30033; (404) 633-2080vwww.communityqbbq.com

This is easily one of the most popular barbecue restaurants in the city. Fans rave about the Pulled pork with its smoky flavor and the tasty brisket. Ribs are juicy and full of meat, and almost don't need either of the two sauces that are found on the tables: sweet, vinegar-based. The Mac n Cheese side gets high marks too. While the wait may not be super long, do expect a fifteen to twenty minute wait on weekends. Note that there isn't table service here. Diners place and pay for orders at the counter, which then brought to their table shortly. Note that the restaurant closes quite early on weekdays at 8:30 and 9:30 on weekends. $$

Desta Ethiopian 3086 Briarcliff Road, Atlanta, GA 30329; (404) 929-0011 www.destaethiopiankitchen.com

You won't find a more popular spot for Ethiopian than Desta, which is the most established. They do have a lovely patio and you should try and sit there whenever possible. Injera is the spongy bread used to soak up the meats and sauces with Ethiopian food. The do offer rice or other bread if you don't want the Injera. The best way to experience this food is to go with a large group and order some of everything (pricing is very affordable). If you are unsure what to order, go for one vegetarian platter and one meat platter. The latter, you can customize with steak, lamb, chicken or fish. If you are not opposed to raw meat, get the Kifto, raw thinly sliced steak with aromatic herbs. There's a private room available for parties. $$

Double Zero 1577 North Decatur Rd. Atlanta, GA 30307; (404) 991-3666 www.doublezeroatl.com

Double Zero gets its name from the flour, "Double Zero" which is imported from Italy and used in the Neapolitan pizza. But there's more than just pizza to this trendy spot. On the menu, find meats and cheeses (build your own charcuterie plate), as well as pastas and full meals. When available get the Pork Belly with Pumpkin Risotto. Some dishes are cooked in the sous vide style, like lamb meatballs. Pizzas are tasty and come with scissors for slicing. $$$

Farm Burger 410B W Ponce de Leon Decatur, GA 30030; (404) 378-5077 www.farmburger.net

This burger spot in the Decatur neighborhood is different in that the ingredients are organic and locally sourced. Fans are more than happy to pay a couple extra dollars to help support local economies and have grass-fed burgers. While it offers up mostly indoor seating, there are a couple tables outside. Customers can build their own burger or order one of the specialty burgers. Unique toppings include Oxtail Marmalade and Roasted Bone Marrow. You must try the house made pickles. For sides, choose onion rings over the fries. Or the Sweet Potato Hushpuppies. Lines can be extremely long. Visit during off peak times for quicker service. $$

The General Muir 1540 Avenue Place, Suite B-230, Atlanta, GA 30329; (678) 927-9131 www.thegeneralmuir.com

For any transplants from the north that were looking for a fabulous deli, I present The General Muir. Open for breakfast, lunch, dinner and brunch on the weekends. For breakfast get the General, pastrami, eggs, latkes and applesauce. At lunch the Reuben or Double Burger is a must. At dinner you can't beat the Poutine. $$

Kimball House 303 East Howard Avenue, Decatur, GA, 30030; (404) 378-3502) www.kimball-house.com

Looking for an aphrodisiac? Head to Kimball House for some of the best oysters in the city. Though you should note, they refuse to take reservations, sort of (the website is a paradox of information on this) which can be a turnoff for some, myself included. But the refurbished train depot, with its penny tile floors and brass and the tufted leather booths, it is rather pretty inside. Go for oysters and a cocktail and then head to one of the other restaurants in Decatur for dinner, if you don't have much time in Atlanta. $$$

Iberian Pig 121 Sycamore St. Decatur, GA 30030; (404) 371-8800 www.theiberianpigatl.com

As the name suggests, this is a Spanish / Mediterranean restaurant. Located in close proximity to the Decatur square, it is a favorite of many that live in the neighborhood. The restaurant gets its name from the Black-footed Iberian Pigs, from which the restaurant's signature item, Jamon Iberico, a cured meat, originate. There's a good selection of meats and cheeses, but the appetizers offer much more in the way of flavor. In fact, many groups treat these as tapas, not ordering any main courses. B.W.D. or Bacon wrapped dates and Pork Cheek Tacos are popular starters. For a more complex appetizer, order the Albondigas – Wild Boar meatballs or Lamb stuffed Piquillo peppers. Skip seafood dishes in favor of meat entrees. $$$

La Brasas 310 E Howard Ave Decatur, GA 30030; (404) 377-9121 www.lasbrasasdecatur.com

Forget those grocery store Rotisserie chickens, and head over to this popular Decatur spot to pick up some Peruvian spiced Rotisserie chicken. This uniquely addictive chicken, was once served as to go only, but popularity encouraged expanding to a full-fledged restaurant. Start your meal with Mixed Ceviche. The signature dish is rotisserie chicken with crispy skin and the juicy meat. Order chicken by the half or full size. Round out your meal with an Inca Kola, a Peruvian style soft drink. The wine selection is limited and not worth the price. $$

Leon's Full Service 131 E. Ponce de Leon Avenue, Decatur, GA 30030; (404) 687-0500 www.leonsfullservice.com

Located in the heart of Decatur, this quasi-gastropub has decent sandwiches and a killer craft beer selection. Start with the pub frites, which come with choice of dipping sauce with flavors like mango-peppadew or chili-sorghum. Sandwiches can be hit or miss. While the Cuban was delicious, a Trout Po Boy was rather disappointing. There is a bocce ball court outside and an inviting patio. They have gluten free and vegetarian menus too. Reservations are not accepted and large tables are hard to come by, so better for couples or small parties. $$

M572 2316 Main St, Tucker, GA 30084; (470) 395-9635 www.fiveseventwo.com

Owner / Chef Jon Allen spent many years working for Chef Kevin Rathbun. M572 is his take on upscale southern cuisine. What's in a name? Before there was the city of Tucker or Dekalb County, Georgia was once carved into militia districts and Tucker was 572, hence the name. A *Beauty School Dropout* cocktail with vodka, Prosecco and lemon shrub is the winner for cocktails. There's a terrific selection of craft beers and an excellently curated wine list, with a large selections of wines by the glass, curated by the chef himself. Start with the fried okra and get the Trout and Grits for an entrée. $$$

Madras Mantra 2179 Lawrenceville Hwy, Decatur, GA 30033; (404) 636-4400 www.madrasmantra.com

Vegetarian never tasted better than at Madras Mantra in Decatur. When you step in Madras Mantra you forget the dingy strip mall exterior. Once you enter you see the exquisite

Indian décor all over. At lunch, buffet service is offered. Dinner is more elegant with waiter service. Start with one of the chat appetizers, which include a mix of yogurt, potatoes, chutney and chickpea noodles or the Samosas. Next get a Dosai (crepe) stuffed with perfectly spiced and fragrant vegetables. $$

Mason Tavern 1371 Clairmont Rd, Decatur, GA 30033; (404) 963-2322 www.masontavernatl.com

Getting its name from the nearby Mason Mill Park, this restaurant has a great interior but a patio is inviting too. The bar is the focal point of the restaurant with flat screens hovering above liquor bottles. For a light and refreshing cocktail, get the Pimm the Tail on the Saint. Standouts are the Poutine with Pork neck and The Jerusalem salad with eggplant, fried artichokes and tahini vinaigrette dressing. The Butcher steak can't be beat either. $$$

No. 246. 129 E Ponce De Leon Ave. Decatur, GA 30030; (678) 399-8246 www.no246.com

Not to let Italian food be part of his restaurant empire, Ford Fry is behind the much beloved No. 246. Pastas and pizzas are stunning. Even simple spaghetti with shrimp is a winner. Pizzas are enough for two to share and are around $20. Often overlooked is the brunch menu. Get the breakfast pizza or, hash or benedict. Planning a special occasion? Book the chef's counter for $50 for a five course menu where you sit overlooking the preparation. Tip: Like Limoncello? Bartenders offer a cello flight of different ingredients. It's perfect for a boozy brunch or before or after dinner. $$$

The Pinewood 254 West Ponce de Leon Ave, Decatur, GA 30030; (404) 373-5507 www.pinewoodtr.com

Much more of a gastropub than neighboring Leon's, the cocktail menu features a mix of classic cocktails and unique ones like Chasing the Rabbit or Fever Dream Ration. Daily lunch specials are available for just $10 -12. At dinner starters like Pork Belly are served with a Jicama salad and pickled watermelon. Octopus comes with white bean puree, and Sun-dried tomato vinaigrette. Entrees like Trout are served with Prosciutto, chili and grilled fennel. $$

Raging Burrito – 141 Sycamore Street, Decatur, GA 30030; (404) 377-3311 www.ragingburrito.com

Patrons don't just flock to this restaurant for the Tex-Mex food, but they've also got a terrific selection of craft beer and delicious margaritas. Burritos like steak, chicken and shrimp can be found, but venture out and try the Pineapple Jerk Chicken, Bangkok, or Tokyo Teriyaki. The lovely patio, complete with Mona Lisa mural, is in high demand when weather is pleasant. $

Revival 129 Church St, Decatur, GA 30030; (470) 225-6770 www.revivaldecatur.com

It doesn't get more southern that Kevin Gillespie's Revival in the heart of Decatur. Establishing roots in a refurbished elegant southern home, great care was taken to keep elements the same like the original windows and hardwood flooring. Artwork on the walls and above the fireplace mantle were created by chef / owner, Kevin Gillespie's grand-mother. The small wine list has been curated with fantastic choices. Though portions are relatively the same, lunch is more affordable than dinner with blue-plate specials offering a main and two sides for well under $20. However, if the southern chowder is available, go for it as it is rarely available at lunch. Skip the Country Fried Steak in favor of Catfish. They offer valet, so forgo the pay lot up the street. They have a lovely beer garden, named Communion, in the back. $$

Saba 350 Meade Rd., Decatur, GA 30030; (404) 377-9266 www.saba-restaurant.com

A great choice for vegetarians, with a plentiful selection of vegetarian dishes like the Vindaloo Tofu Spaghetti and Thai Ravioli with peanut and cilantro sauce, the menu skews towards Italian. Meat eaters will enjoy the hearty sausage sandwich, served on ciabatta buns. Tip: The restaurant is kid-friendly early evenings, but when live music begins later, it's time to get the kiddies to bed. $$

Sprig 2860 Lavista Rd, Decatur, GA 30033; (404) 248-9700 www.sprigrestaurant.com

The unassuming restaurant is hiding a secret – one of the best bourbon lists in the city. Start your meal off with Grit Sticks, complete with Romanesco sauce. Another mark of any terrific southern restaurant is pimento cheese and theirs is served with bacon tomato jam. Portions are large for the price. A standout on the menu is the Lamb Stroganoff.

Tip: There's a lovely park next door. Here, you can get your cocktail to go (totally legal here) and walk around the park. The patio is dog friendly too. $$$

Sun in My Belly   2161 College Ave. Atlanta, GA 30317; (404) 370-1088 www.suninmybelly.com

The Kitschy restaurant was once a hardware store and the old signage still exists on the restaurant's front entrance. The sparse décor features butcher paper on the tables and drinks are served out of mason jars. The front of the restaurant has couches for lounging and the large mugs of coffee make you want to lounge there and read or work on your laptop. At breakfast and lunch, the Kirkwood Breakfast is the way to go, with scrambled eggs with Boursin cheese, served with bacon and biscuits. Sweets lovers should get the Challah French Toast which is made with honeyed ricotta and berries. At lunch you can't go wrong with the fried green tomato sandwich or the cumin spiked hummus. They also have a lovely supper club dinner Thursday through Saturdays: 4 courses for $40. $$

Tava Indian Bistro 1685 Church Street, Decatur, GA 30033; (404) 343-2710 www.tavaindianbistro.com

Farm to Table is not what you'd expect from an Indian restaurant, but that's what Tava does. The brainchild of Emory University student Farhan Momin, his family owns the butch shop in the same plaza. The decor modern looking with faux wood walls and an overall minimalist style. The east meets west style of food features items like Bihari Chicken Wings (pictured above), covered with Indian spices. The special of the house, a Nihari Sandwich minced lamb is fabulous, with specially seasoned meat and on bread sourced from a special bakery. Beat the heat of the spicy dishes with Nimboo Pani, sweet lemonade with a hint of cumin. $$

Wahoo! Decatur Grill 1042 West College Avenue Decatur, GA 30030; 404-373-3331 www.wahoogrilldecatur.com

The layout of the restaurant is interesting in that they have 3 different seating areas: indoors, enclosed patio and outside.

Inside, the small wood tables which give a view to the open kitchen. Ask for a seat on the enclosed patio consisting of a brick floor with views of outdoors. Seafood is the star of the show here with items like Florida Grouper, Scallops and Faroe Island Salmon. Tip: They have a market next door to the restaurant (Wahoo Wine and Provisions), which includes many locally sourced items like meats, cheeses and even wine growlers. So, it you are in a hurry, you can make a meal of the many items to choose from. $$$

CHAPTER 7
Buford Highway

The Buford Highway area of Atlanta is where most of our truly ethnic restaurants are located. Located slightly north of the city, Atlantans trek out to Buford Highway in search of the latest and greatest new find. Many different ethnicities are represented along Buford Highway. Here you'll find Chinese, Korean, Mexican, and Vietnamese among others. As one would expect the food is not only authentic but prices are low, as these establishments are not located in high rent areas and décor is kept to a minimum. It is not uncommon to have a fantastic and filling meal for fewer than ten dollars. Part of the fun of Buford Highway is getting out and exploring all there is to offer and knowing that you just might stumble on that next great restaurant. Note that many of these restaurants pick a strange day to close like Tuesdays or Wednesdays. So, check online or contact the restaurant before visiting.

A-Priori 5953 Buford Hwy, Doraville, GA 30340; (678) 978-3174

The seafood heavy restaurant is a departure from most no frills Buford Highway spots, the white tablecloths not something you would expect from the outside strip mall view. The menu is an eclectic mix of both Asian and Russian items. Though the appetizers aren't cheap (probably around $15 each), they do offer a generous serving, that could easily work as an entree. Get the Octopus or Mussels appetizer to start. A Corn Arugula salad is delicious with Feta and basil vinaigrette making it more spectacular. Lamb chops or fish Entrees are terrific. Closed Mondays and Tuesdays. $$$

Bo Bo Garden 5181 Buford Hwy Atlanta, GA 30340; (678) 547-1881

For terrific Chinese food, Bo Bo Garden will satisfy. Bring all your friends and order family style as the huge round tables are perfect for groups. Start off you meal with the Three Kinds Dumpling soup. For mains get the Spare Ribs and Taro. The ribs have delicious an addictive sauce. The Taro is quite interesting as well, cubed and served in a cream sauce. If you love lobster, this an excellent choice with it being quite affordable here. $$

Canton House 4825 Buford Hwy Atlanta, GA 30341; (770) 936-9030 www.cantonhouserestaurant.com

For those in search of decent Dim Sum, you'll want to pay a visit to Canton House, although you can have a perfectly decent non-Dim Sum meal here as well. Order the Pork Shu Mai. Slather the chili sauce over top and it is brilliant with the savory pork pieces inside. Another hit are the steamed spare ribs. Try to arrive by 11am, or anytime later than that you may be waiting for a table as this is a very popular restaurant within the Atlanta Chinese population. $

Chef Liu 5221 Buford Hwy Atlanta, GA 30340; (770) 936-0532 www.chefliuatlanta.com

Known for their soup dumplings, everyone falls in love with them when they visit. The Shanghai Juicy Steamed Pork Buns are truly incredible but be careful as the soup is very hot. Many a customer favorite is the Leek Pie, which is more pancake than pie. The Lamb Kabobs are a must order as well. You'll get several skewers for under $5! Closed Wednesdays. $

Chateau Saigon 4300 Buford Hwy Ste 218 Atlanta, GA 30345; (404) 929-0034 www.chateaudesaigon.com

Upon entering, you'll notice that this establishment has a much more beautiful interior than some of its other Buford Highway neighbors. Start your meal with the Salt and Pepper Calamari as well as the Papaya salad. The perfectly prepared calamari is tender with a light batter. The Shaking Beef and the Spicy Lemongrass Chicken are also fantastic entrée options. My favorite is the Crispy Egg Noodles, with both meat and seafood. Of course, you can't go wrong with Pho here. And a Lemongrass Tofu dish is so tasty, even carnivores will devour it! $$

Chong Qing Hot Pot 5385 New Peachtree Rd Atlanta, GA 30341; (770) 936-1379

Located in the food court of the Chinatown Mall, this is truly no frills, but that doesn't mean people won't drive far for their delicious hot pots, which are spiced to your preference. You can't go wrong with either the seafood or pork hot pot. But do be sure and sample one of the non-pot dishes too. My recommendation is the Cumin Lamb. Tip: They offer free tea and soup with your meal purchase. They only accept cash. $

Cho Dang Tofu House 5907 Buford Hwy Atlanta, GA 30340; (770) 220-0667

Don't let the name fool you, there are plenty of meat-centric dishes to be found on the menu, even if Tofu soup is the star here. If you aren't looking to get soup, Bulgogi is spectacular and the Seafood Pancake is as well but beware that it is quite spicy. On a hot Atlanta day, the Cold Noodles are perfection. If the drive to Buford Highway is a long one, make an afternoon of it and get a food massage at Treat Your Feet, located across the street. Tip: They offer free ice cream and coffee with the purchase of your meal. $

Com Vietnamese 4005 Buford Hwy Ste E Atlanta, GA 30345; (404) 320-0405 www.comgrillrestaurant.com

Com is perfect for those seeking non-Pho Vietnamese food. When headed to Com be on the lookout or you could easily miss it. Behind a gas station, it's difficult to spot from the road. Give the flat rice vermicelli a try. Another great option is the duck stuffed grape leaves. The most popular dish here is the Com Special, a dish with rice, an egg, a shrimp-crab cake, and choice of meat. Waiters here speak excellent

English, so no language barrier issues to be feared whatsoever. Their corkage fee is negligible, so feel free to bring a bottle of your choosing and enjoy. $$

Crawfish Shack 4337 Buford Hwy #170, Atlanta, GA 30341; (404) 329-1610 www.crawfishshackseafood.com

With its strip mall location, it's far less "shack" than the name suggests and the food is mighty tasty. The uniqueness is the Cajun food with a Vietnamese influence. Besides crawfish, seafood items are plentiful, but my favorite is the fried shrimp. If you want a taste of everything, get the Shack-tastic platter. They have Beignets on the menu, but they've been sold out each time I've visited. Tip: Want to cook crawfish at home? They sell it by the pound for $8. $$

Dong Ne Bang Ne 3042 Oakcliff Road, Suite 104, Doraville, GA 30340; (770) 458-1552

The name of this Korean Barbecue spot means "Kimchi House". You would never know it existed, being located behind another restaurant, completely hidden from sight on Buford Highway. The All You Can Eat barbecue, which many visit here for is about $19 per person. For something different, order the Summer Stamina Goat Hotpot (Yeomsul Chongul). Because of the effort involved in this dish it is only available for groups. This comes with Banchan (Korean sides) which included 2 kinds of kimchi, mushrooms, tiny shrimp (with shells on), rice, etc. The goat is delicious (not spicy) and, unlike most places, the goat is served boneless. $$

El Ray Del Taco 5288 Buford Hwy Atlanta, GA 30340; (770) 986-0032

This fun loving restaurant is open every day from 10 am to 5 am! If you are looking for unique meats like Lengua (Beef Tongue), Cabeza (Beef Cheek) to name a few, you will find them here. Asada is excellent too. The Corn tortillas are hand made with and slightly charred for a pretty appearance. Start your meal off with their sensational guacamole. They are vegetarian friendly as well offering several non-meat tacos like mushroom and bean. Note that the service charge is included in the check, so no need to tip. $

Hae Woon Dae 5805 Buford Hwy Atlanta, GA 30340; (770) 451-7957 $$

While the prices for this Korean BBQ may be a little pricier than other options nearby, the quality is extremely high. Part of the difference in quality of Hae Woon Dae over other Korean BBQ joints elsewhere in the city, is that their grills are charcoal vs. the gas grills. This difference of using the charcoal over gas gives the meat a smokiness that isn't found in other restaurants. They are open late night every day from 11 am to 6 am. Wednesdays they close at midnight. $$$

Harmony Vegetarian 4897 Buford Hwy Ste 109 Atlanta, GA 30341; (770) 457-7288

While this establishment only serves vegetarian food, they serve up many, many mock meat entrees. They use imitation product to make entrees with beef, pork, and poultry. It is not only a haven for vegetarians, but serves some wonderful Chinese dishes as well. Soups like Hot and Sour and Wonton are extremely popular with vegetarians and omnivores alike. Mongolian Beef and Sesame Chicken are very tasty here.

Vegetarians and vegans will be pleased to be able to order from the entire menu and not just a small portion. Closed Tuesdays $

Havana Restaurant 3979 Buford Hwy Ste 108 Atlanta, GA 30319; (404) 633-7549 www.havanaatlanta.com

Cuban food fans were wholeheartedly disappointed when one of the most popular Cuban joints in Atlanta, Kool Korners, closed its doors. Thanks goodness for Havana restaurant, which has no doubt filled some of that void. Portions here are huge. Two could easily split a sandwich, which comes with rice and beans. Plantains, Yucca and Empanadas are all excellent here. Opt for chicken empanadas over pork. This restaurant gets quite crowded at lunch time. But for take-out orders, food is ready quickly. Note that they close early on Sundays: 7pm. $

Lee's Bakery 4005 Buford Hwy Atlanta, GA 30345; (404) 728-1008

The Pho is solid, but if you like Banh Mi sandwiches, here's where to find the best in the city. They even have a combo of half sandwich and order of Pho reasonably priced. The restaurant is extremely clean and the ingredients are extremely high quality – sprouts, mint, cilantro, jalapenos everything is fresh. The Banh Mi with pork is tender and the combination of crunchy vegetables and spicy jalapenos make bite after bite supremely delicious. For a drink, order the Avocado smoothie or Bubble Tea. $

Little Szechwan 5091 Buford Hwy Atlanta, GA 30340; (770) 451-0192 www.littleszechuanatlanta.com

Some find traditional Chinese food too salty or heavy on the sauce. At Little Szechwan they do go light on the salt and sauce here. Portions are rather large and unless you're starving, one entrée will easily make for two to three meals. Vegetarian entrees can be found on the menu, but the better dishes are meat-oriented, with the exception of Eggplant. If you like Eggplant, they offer several dishes where this vegetable shines. Bring cash, as they accept credit cards but are reluctant to take them as payment. $$

Mamak 5150 Buford Hwy Doraville, GA 30340; (678) 395-3192 www.mamak-kitchen.com

Malaysian restaurants aren't plentiful in Atlanta, so Mamak is a welcome addition to Buford Highway. The small space has a pretty big menu. For starters, get the Roti Canai, an Indian type bread with curry sauce. If you're playing it safe get the Hainanese Chicken. If you are feeling more adventurous get the fish head curry. A traditional dish that is crowd-pleaser, is the Chow Kway Teow. The flat rice noodles are stir-fried and served sans any broth. $$

Man Chung Hong 5953 Buford Hwy Ste 105 Atlanta, GA 30340; (770) 454-5640

Unusual, but this restaurant seems to be a mix of both Chinese and Korean. There's complimentary tea and Kimchee. As the restaurant specializes in Sichuan dishes, the Dry Fried Eggplant or Twice cooked Pork are exceptional dishes. For the more authentic food, make sure to ask for a Sichuan menu. Skip dumplings in favor of noodle dishes, like the Black Bean Noodles. Some guests even enjoy watching the noodles being made. The restaurant does get very busy on Friday and Saturday night, so expect a wait at peak times. Tip: If you do have a large group, they take reservations. Closed Mondays. $

Ming's Bar B Que 5150 Buford Hwy # 300 Doraville, GA 30340; (770) 451-6985

Walking by Ming's Bar Que, you'll be lured in the by glistening and crispy looking meats hanging on display in the window. It is reminiscent of some of the very Chinese restaurants that are located in New York City's Chinatown. Crispy duck and the BBQ are the real reasons to come here. Congee (rice porridge) lovers will appreciate this dish here. The rice pairs well with the rich flavors of the meat it is served alongside. Tip: When I visit Buford Highway, I always get a crispy duck from Ming's to take home and have another day. It's a deal at just $20 plus they chop it for you as well. They only accept cash here. $

Nam Phuong 4051 Buford Hwy Atlanta, GA 30345; (404) 633-2400

While you can get Pho and Banh Mi at this Vietnamese restaurant, there are plenty of other tasty dishes that warrant trying as well. Start with the Papaya salad and add chicken or shrimp. Beef dishes are excellent here. I'd focus on the Shaking Beef or the Beef Stew with a rich sauce and served with bread or egg noodles. Tip: The restaurant is BYOB and there is no corkage fee. There's a second location (the original) in Norcross. $

Panahar 3375 Buford Hwy Suite 1060 Atlanta, GA 30329; (404) 633-6655 www.panahar.com

Although Bangladeshi cuisine is not very prominent in Atlanta, this is a fantastic representation of it. Chutneys are quite delicious like the Peach or Spicy Onion. Garlic Naan and Onion Naan are two of the best flavors, but even the plain Naan is tasty. There are many vegetarian options and a couple stand out dishes are Dharosh bhaaji - sauteed okra with onion, tomatoes, and herbs or the Vegetable Korma. Chicken Tikka should not be missed. The food is as flavorful as Indian, but not as hot and spicy. Also, you can BYOB with no corkage fees. Fridays and Saturdays get busy so reservations are a must. Closed Mondays $$

Pho Dai Loi 4186 Buford Hwy #G Atlanta, GA 30345; (404) 633-2111

The Pho here is quite amazing as it is hearty with lots of meat and the broth is extremely flavorful as well. Order the Pho Dac Biet (the pho with everything - all the meats, yo). If you are not a fan of Pho, they also have Vermicelli bowls or rice dinners. Food comes out quickly and service is prompt. So, this could most certainly be a stop on the lunch hour. They serve Vietnamese coffee and Bubble Tea too. $

Quoc Huong 5150 Buford Hwy Atlanta, GA 30340; (770) 936-0605

Quoc Huong serves up some of the best Banh Mi sandwiches in town. The New York Times agrees as they wrote it up in an article detailing the best Banh Mi sandwiches in the country. The combination of the crispy and buttered Baguette with the quality meat and veggies make this sandwich superb. Tip: Buy five and get one free. Cash only. Closed Thursdays. $

Royal China 3295 Chamblee Dunwoody Rd, Chamblee, GA 30341; (770) 216-9933

The Chinese restaurant is designed for large groups and that's the best way to enjoy their food. While dishes at lunch and dinner are good, most people know this is where to come for stellar Dim Sum. The different carts being pushed around are a feast for the eyes. Some highlights are the shrimp and pork dumplings, tripe and turnip cakes. If you are feeling adventurous, order the chicken feet. Make sure to arrive before noon or you will be waiting.

So Kong Dong Tofu House 5280 Buford Hwy #C Atlanta, GA 30340 (678) 205-0555

They make an excellent tofu soup. Staff is here is friendly and a majority of the servers do speak English well enough to provide good service. Kalbi and Bibimbap are stand out dishes. The banchan (side dishes served with the main meal) are plentiful. $$

Sushi House Hayakawa 5979 Buford Hwy Ste A-10 Atlanta, GA 30340; (770) 986-0010 www.atlantasushibar.com

Although it is one of the more expensive Buford Highway restaurants, this is the real deal. Some sushi restaurants try to impress with trendy décor or loud dance music, but that's not what you'll find at Sushi House Hayakawa. The well-trained chef knows his stuff. That is why most choose the Omakase, or Chef's choice, instead of ordering their own. Regulars like to sit at the sushi bar and watch as the chef prepares their sushi. For those that aren't sushi fans, the noodle bowls are quite good too. Reservations are a must on Fridays and Saturdays. Closed on Mondays and Tuesdays. Good selection of Sake. $$$

Woo Nam Jeong Stone Bowl House Seoul Plaza 5953
Buford Hwy Ste 107 Atlanta, GA 30340; (678) 530-0844

The décor at Woo Nam Jeong Stone Bowl is a cut above the
rest of the dining establishments in and along the Buford
Highway Corridor. The Dolsot Bimbimbap (Stone Soup) is
comparable to what you can find in New York City. These
bowls are still sizzling when placed in front of you. If you
visit with a group order the Nine Treasure Plate (Gujeolpan)
and Steamed Black Pork Belly with Kimchi and Oysters (Bo
Ssam). The plethora of banchan (sides) is a glorious and full
of different tastes and textures. In addition, there is also a
multi-course tasting menu available, which is upwards of
twelve courses. The chief cook, aka "Grandma", a very sweet
old lady, often greets large parties. If you are lucky she'll
make some cinnamon tea for you. $$

CHAPTER 8
Sandy Springs and Dunwoody

Sandy Springs has been noted as one of the most affluent zip codes in the country. Besides many multi-million dollars homes in the area, there is much new construction with lots of brick and stone. Residents like their specialty markets and bakeries. Businesses have also moved out into these areas as well. So expect to find high end, pricier restaurants that cater to this crowd.

Alon's 505 Ashford Dunwoody Rd Atlanta, GA 30346; (678) 397-1781 www.alons.com

Alon's Bakery & Market's menu highlights international selections derived by Chef and owner Alon Balshan's travels and experiences (he grew up in Israel and studied European cuisine). Items are made fresh daily and can be savored at the restaurant or on-the-go. The European style market, Alon's has a wide selection of baked breads, European-style cakes, handmade pastries, gourmet sandwiches, freshly prepared foods, fine cheeses, exquisite chocolates and even wine. Tip: They make incredible French Macarons! $

Bishoku Sushi 5920 Roswell Rd, Ste B-111, Sandy Springs, GA 30342; (404) 252-7998 www.bishokusushi.com

The sleek interior is perfect for a date night. The sushi bar is the focal point of the restaurant. Lunch has rather limited selections, so it's better to visit for dinner if you want more than a standard bento box. At dinner, sushi like Salmon and Toro are standouts as well as the Tuna. You can't go wrong with the Tonkatsu Ramen either. If you enjoy Sake, the selection here is rather vast. $$

Breadwinners 220 Sandy Springs Cir Atlanta, GA 30328; (404) 843-0224 www.breadwinnercafe.com

As the name suggests, the restaurant sells bread. But these loaves are more of a dessert than those that would be used for a sandwich. The variety is tremendous and these breads theses breads have funky names like the "Papa Don't Peach" or the "Party at My Place Pumpkin". Although the loaves are pricey at $15, they are quite tasty. Many choose to get the 3 pack variety which comes in a gift box and wrapped in bow, to give as gifts around the holidays. They also have a café that serves soups, salads, and sandwiches with many gluten free and vegetarian offerings. Sandwiches like the Caprese or Tuna Melt with tomatoes, Muenster cheese are menu highlights. They are a great choice for catering too. Closed Sundays. $

Cibo E Beve 4969 Roswell Road, Ste 245 Atlanta, GA 30342; (404) 250-8988 www.ciboatlanta.com

The name literally means "Eat and Drink," the Italian spot is a perfect choice for a date night or an intimate gathering of friends. For starters, you'll find items like Crispy Brussels with smoked bacon and poached egg and Honey Compressed

Watermelon with smoked paprika mascarpone. They also have pizza and the signature is the Brooklyn, made with house made sausage. Another signature item is the Lobster Spaghetti. Serviced with minimal seasoning, it is quite the lobster lover's special. Of course, Italians classics like Chicken Piccata and Osso Buco are on the menu as well. $$$

Cowfish 4400 Ashford Dunwoody Road, Atlanta, GA 30346; (770) 225-0009 www.thecowfish.com

A popular trendy restaurant which hails from Charlotte, the Cowfish is located in Perimeter Mall. A contrasting menu is made up of sushi and burgers. Though the look of the restaurant may seem gimmicky, the sushi options are quite upscale and the presentation, beautiful. Get the Big Al's Yellowtail. Sliced razor thin, it is perfection when dipped into the Ponzu sauce that comes with the dish. Can't decide on what type of fish you want? Get the Chef's Deluxe 15 Piece Sashimi at the Cowfish which comes with tuna, salmon, yellowtail, shrimp and octopus. A Tropical Storm roll is tasty too. The Dynamic Duo burger, with braised short rib and tomato onion jam is the jam. The signature here is Burgushi, burgers made into sushi. It's a novelty but may be appealing to kids. Stick with either burgers or sushi. Tip: They have daily specials, many just $2, included a Camel burger. $$

Five Seasons Brewing 5600 Roswell Rd Atlanta, GA 30342; (404) 255-5911   5seasonsbrewing.com

Five Seasons is a unique restaurant, not only specializing in their own unique brews, but the restaurant also boasts an organic menu. Beer aficionados will appreciate the offerings which change regularly. The menu is much better than what can be found at a standard pub. Start with the Grilled Shrimp and Grit Cake or the Alligator Eggrolls. Their pizzas, offered on a thin-crust are quite tasty as well (think granny smith apples and serrano ham), and menu highlights are the Duck Breast and Rabbit Enchiladas. There's even a large patio for group functions or get-togethers. Reservations suggested for weekends. $$$

Food 101 4969 Roswell Rd #200, Atlanta, GA 30342; (404) 497-9700 www.food101atl.com

The modern Southern cuisine is served in an upscale atmosphere. At dinner, the Squash blossoms or the Green Tomato Gazpacho are a must. For mains get the Pulled Pork Enchilada or Short Ribs. At lunch get the Three Meat Meatloaf, Hawaiian Ripper (Kobe beef hot dog with bacon, and a pineapple jalapeno relish). The lobster roll doesn't disappoint either. Tip: The Barrel Bar, Food 101's bar features both classic and New Southern cocktails as well as happy hour nosh like Chicken and Waffles and Reuben Sliders. $$$

Genki Sushi 5590 Roswell Rd Ste 100 Atlanta, GA 30342; (404) 843-8319 www.genki-inc.com

This popular sushi spot is located in the Prado shopping center, which is in the heart of Sandy Springs. Order a mango martini or Red Samurai from the bar. For starters don't miss the Hamachi Kama (Yellowtail) which is crispy on the outside and tender and flaky on the inside, or any of the Tuna appetizers. Seaweed salad is also worth trying. Note that there are a number of cooked entrees and noodle bowls at Genki as well, so a perfectly fine choice for non-sushi enthusiasts as well. $$

Hammock's Trading Company 7285 Roswell Rd. Sandy Springs. GA 30328; (770) 395-9592 www. hammockstrad-ingcompany.com

With a chef that got his training from Wolfgang Puck, you'll want to visit this under the radar spot immediately. Classic cocktails like a Horse's Neck and the Negroni are made perfectly and are reasonably priced. Get the barbecued oysters or Trout Salad to start. Any seafood entrees are terrific like the Scallops (perfectly done and served with a sweet Risotto) or Flounder. Presentation is beautiful here. And for dessert, save room for the Campfire S'mores if you're dining with a group. $$$

Hearth Pizza 5992 Roswell Road, Sandy Springs, GA 30328; (404) 252-5378; www.hearthpizzatvern.com

Pizza is baked in a 600 degree hearth oven, hence the name. The beer selection is decent with over 10 on draft and more than double that by the bottle. Their Brussels Sprouts are a delicious appetizer to start with, the balsamic adding a sweet match to the salty bacon. The best pizzas are the Ring of Fire with chile oil, chorizo, cilantro, roasted mushrooms as well as the Mass Pike with Italian Sausage, pesto, mushrooms and sundried tomatoes. $$

Henri's Bakery 6289 Roswell Rd Atlanta, GA 30328; (404) 256-7934 www.henrisbakery.com

This bakery has treats of cookies, cakes, tarts and desserts of all kinds. Most are lured in by the tasty treats and but opt for a meal when they eye the deli with made-to-order sandwiches. Most sandwiches are served on onion rolls that are heavenly. The Roast Beef Po Boy Sandwich, Turkey Sandwich or Egg / Chicken /Tuna sandwiches are all tasty. They offer many small pastries that are too tempting to not add to your lunch order. Try their Petit-Fours: four small slices of cake, which are incredible. $

Horseradish Grill 4320 Powers Ferry Rd Atlanta, GA 30342; (404) 255-7277 www.horseradishgrill.com

This restaurant has been popular with Atlanta residents for many years. Located rather close to the Chastain Park Amphitheatre, it is a popular choice before concerts in the open-air amphitheater. Start with the Tempura fried Okra. Their signature dish is their Fried Chicken, which many visiting from out of town are big fans. Steaks, Grouper or Georgia Trout are all solid choices. While the interior of the restaurant is classy and well-appointed, the patio is secluded with trees and plants surrounding it and well worth spending an evening dinner. They are quite popular for brunch too. $$$$

MAYA Steaks and Seafood 6152 Roswell Rd, Atlanta, GA 30328; (404) 705-8880 www.mayasteaks.com

MAYA has over 40 wines by the glass, all chosen by MAYA's owner, Mimmo Alboumeh. He's owner of Red Pepper Taqueria restaurants, known for their locally sourced organic ingredients. But MAYA reflects his time spent in both Spain and Italy. MAYA, named after his youngest daughter, brings his passion for multiple cuisines to fruition. Start with the Crispy Lobster Tail and Beef Carpaccio (sliced daily). A very light batter covers the perfectly succulent lobster tail.

Steaks are the star of the menu with choices of Filet, Veal Porterhouse, Ribeye and NY Strip supplied from Braveheart Black Angus Beef Purveyors. Top your steak with the simple "M Sauce". The intimate atmosphere is perfect for a romantic evening. $$$$

Memphis BBQ Company 4764 Ashford-Dunwoody Rd Atlanta, GA 30338; (770) 394-7427 www.memphisbbqco. com

The restaurant was started by Melissa Cookston, who's won numerous awards for her barbecue and is a cookbook author. You must order of the cheese balls to start. More than the 4 cheeses used, it is the honey Dijon dipping sauce that sets it apart from other dishes. Though there are fish, chicken and shrimp 'n grits on the menu, the award winning barbecue is the way to go. They smoke their barbecue for 16 hours a day over pecan wood, resulting in the pink "smoke-ring" look. Order one of their MBC Platters, like the Grand Champion which comes with chicken, brisket, sausage, and pulled pork, baby back and spare ribs. This platter could feed about six people and is an excellent value at just about $50. This gigantic platter is served in a garbage can lid! $$

Nori Nori 6690 Roswell Rd Sandy Springs, GA 30328; (404) 257-1288 www.norinori.com

Most sushi lovers may not be fans of a buffet, but this buffet is quite fresh and staff brings out new offerings quickly. Besides sushi there are many other foods offered here like salads, oysters, crab legs, chicken dishes and desserts. Dinner buffet offers a wider selection of goods. Lunch buffet is nearly half the price, but still not cheap by any means. Make sure to explore all areas of the buffet area as it is large and you'll want to make sure to be aware of all the goods that are available. $$

Rumi's Kitchen 6152 Roswell Rd Atlanta, GA 30328; (404) 477-2100 www.rumiskitchen.com

The décor is pretty upscale, which sets this Persian restaurant apart from some of its counterparts in the area. Upon being seated, the table is treated to a complimentary plate of plate of bread with walnuts, olives, feta, radishes, and mint. Start the meal off with kashk badenjoon and hummus. Kabobs of shrimp or chicken are quite tasty and have tangy kick to them. The Lamb Shank is a customer favorite. Note: there are not Vegetarian options here. Reservations required. $$$

Taka Sushi 4600 Roswell Rd E110, Sandy Springs, GA 30342; (404) 851-1500 www.takasushiatlanta.com

Taka was a favorite in Buckhead, before moving to Sandy Springs recently. For those seeking variety and a tasting of many different items, opt for the 8-course omakase. Omakase is a chef's choice as far as selection. One of the menu highlights is the Hamachi Kami (Yellowtail Cheek) of which there are only a couple available every day but it is prepared excellently and is very meaty. Service is on point, with servers able to make suggestions and happy to bring Sake samples to taste. For drinks, choose from 30+ wines and premium sake from the Wine Spectator award-winning list. Tips: Closed on Sundays. $$$

Three Sheets 6017 Sandy Springs Circle, Atlanta, GA 30328; (404) 303-8423 www.threesheetsatlanta.com

The upscale lounge boasts specialty nights like the Grilled Cheese and wine pairing once a month and the Flavor tripping event. Grilled Cheese night's features five different kinds of grilled cheese paired with different wines. Think of Machego, mushrooms, truffle aioli on sourdough paired with Pinot Noir. Flavor Tripping events send your taste buds into a tailspin, turning sour lemons into a sweet lemonade flavor and goat cheese to a sweet cheesecake. Weekends skew towards an older (read: cougar) crowd. Small plates are items like hummus, falafel, charcuterie and flatbreads. But you can get heartier dishes like scallops and seabass, but keep in mind this is a lounge and it can get awkward to eat larger plates with them in your lap. $$$

Teela Taqueria 227 Sandy Spring Place Suite 506 Sandy Springs, GA 30328; (404) 459-0477 www.teelataqueria.com

Fun is the best way to describe Teela Taqueria. Located in the City Walk center, this lively and bright Taqueria is just the kind of restaurant that the shopping center needed. Specialty drinks here are mojitos and margaritas. Start off with the trio of salsa, guacamole and cheese dip. Bang Bang Shrimp (shrimp with a chili aioli) and the Shrimp and Crab (crab and shrimp cake with chipotle cream cheese) tacos are a must for seafood lovers. The Southern BLT taco is interesting as well – bacon, lettuce and *fried green* (that's where the Southern part comes in) tomatoes with feta cheese and smoky chili aioli. But the Chorizo taco is divine, the marriage of spicy chorizo, with salty feta, sweet dates is a perfect combination. For dessert, you can't go wrong with Tres Leches or Flan. $

Tin Can Fish House and Oyster Bar 227 Sandy Spring Place Suite 502 Sandy Springs, GA 30328; (404) 497 9997 www.tincanfishhouse.com

Located just next door to Teela Taqueria , this rustic looking seafood establishment is its sister restaurant. Diners can even order off either restaurant's menu. The décor evokes memories of past visits to beachy waterfront cafes. If the decor doesn't make you feel like you just stepped off the boardwalk, the food sure will. Starters of Mussels in cilantro-coconut curry or the Ahi Tuna are all hits. The menu has Po Boys, for those so inclined, but for only a few dollars more, get the fish, prepared to your liking with two sides. While preparation can be blackened, sweet chili glazed, horseradish crusted and the always popular fried, the most popular seems to be Blackened Grouper or Mahi Mahi. $$

Tupelo Honey Café 4600 Roswell Road #110, Sandy Springs, GA 30342; (404) 649-6334 www.tupelohoneycafe.com

An order of biscuits is a must. It might sound trite – ordering made-from-scratch biscuits at a Southern restaurant, but trust me when I tell you these flaky biscuits are incredible, only made better by the house made blueberry jam slathered on top of them. Starters outshine entrees here. You can't go wrong with The Fried Green Tomatoes, Shrimp Tacos, Scallop Sofrito, and Chipotle Wings. But the fried chicken is quite impressive. Tip: They have a pretty decent wine and craft beer list and the specialty

Mule cocktail of the month is priced right at just $5. $$$

Under the Cork Tree 5600 Roswell Rd #2, Sandy Springs, GA 30342; (678) 827-2842 www.corktreerestaurant.com

Dark wood, leather sofas and gorgeous chandeliers are found at this Sandy Springs restaurant, located in the Prado Shopping center. The patio has comfortable seating, complete with heaters for cool evenings, and perfect for sipping on wine and noshing on small plates on date or girls night. As with any Spanish tapas restaurant, charcuterie selection is plentiful. But there are also two dozen tapas. The sweet and salty Medjool Dates and Albondigas (veal and pork meatballs) are a good start. Octopus a la Plancha and Lamb Ribs are great choices too. Note: the majority of the tapas are gluten free. While the restaurant is appropriate for a special occasion, it doesn't have to be a pricey evening. Pastas and pizzas are also available, priced under $15. $$$

Villa Christina 4000 Summit Boulevard, Brookhaven, GA 30319 (678) 539-1234 www.villachristina.com

Though the address may be Brookhaven, it is rather close to Dunwoody. The restaurant, attached to a Hyatt is a hidden back behind an apartment complex. Salads are large and lovely. Get the feta with roasted red peppers. A Sea Bass or Red Snapper with risotto are menu highlights. Menu pricing is surprisingly reasonable for hotel dining. Tip: They have incredible pizzas baked in their wood oven, but you'll have to order them at the bar as they are not listed on the menu. $$$

Wright's Gourmet Sandwich 5482 Chamblee Dunwoody Rd, Dunwoody, GA 30338; (770) 396-7060 www.wrightgourmetshoppe.com

You'll see the menu listed on two huge blackboards that you can't miss when you enter the restaurant. Try the New Orleans classic, Muffuletta, oozing with cheese and very hearts. The Rebel Reuben, made with turkey, is also a customer favorite. Skip the side of chips in favor of their house-made sides like potato or broccoli salad. Desserts like the lemonade cake are irresistible. The restaurant also offers catering of boxed lunches as well as cakes and pies. They are not open for dinner and are closed on Sundays. $

CHAPTER 9
Worth the Drive

This section highlights notable restaurants located outside the city's perimeter. As locals know the ITP (Inside the Perimeter) folks, often look down with disdain at anything OTP (Outside the Perimeter). However, these carefully selected restaurants have something exceptional that makes them worth a long drive.

Aqua Blue 1564 Holcomb Bridge Rd Roswell, GA 30076; (770) 643 8886 www.aquablueatl.com

It's sleek, modern interior could fool you into thinking you were in an upscale Midtown restaurant. Behind the hostess stand is a large bar area with plenty of high tops, and as beautiful as it is, you could enjoy your entire meal there. The main dining area is pretty snazzy itself, with white booths and nicely appointed light fixtures, and of course the cozy patio beckons on warm evenings. Skip cocktails and dive right into the wine list. Servers can help with wine recommendations. Start with the calamari, Tempura Green Beans and crab cake. Ask for the half and half options of Calamari and Green Beans as the portions are huge. The Sea Bass and King Clip Fish are quite delicious, with the slightly crunch exterior giving way to the buttery insides. $$$

Aqua Terra Bistro 55 E Main St Buford, GA 30518; (770) 271-3000 www.aquaterrabistro.com

Chef Brian Legault has been churning out fantastic dishes to Buford folks for years. Ask to be seated in the funky cellar dining area. Start your meal with the Potato Eggrolls. A rare Unicorn Fish served with orange ginger aioli is delicious. But the signature Scallops, over orecchiette with a mushroom truffle cream sauce that has never left the menu is a must. The charming space with its exposed brick walls and beams and bamboo flooring, it a good spot for a date or a private party. $$$

Atlantic Seafood Company 2345 Mansell Rd Alpharetta, GA 30022; (770) 640-0488 www.atlanticseafoodco.com

Atlantic Seafood Company has a mammoth menu to match is expansive, upscale space. It is not uncommon to find many business diners on weeknights. Start with a Seaweed Salad or a Squid Salad, then follow it up with the crab and bacon

oysters. Traditional sushi Rolls like Spicy Tuna, Rainbow and Dynamite are all to be found. But I recommend the Psychedelic one, made with tuna, salmon, and the most delicious combination of curry aioli, eel sauce and scallion oil. Chilean seabass with wasabi beurre blanc will round out your seafood dining experience quite nicely. Don't think about skipping dessert, specifically the Orange-Creamsicle Panna Cotta. Pair that with the specialty Atlantic Seafood Company Cappuccino with crème de cacao and brandy and that is one sweet ending. They offer a decent variety of gluten-free menu items. $$$

Bistro VG 70 W Crossville Rd Roswell, GA 30075; (770) 993-1156 www.bistrovg.com

The mostly white décor, walls and tables, etc, give the overall feel of a modern minimalist look, but the off-white French fabrics on chairs lend a little warmth to the overall feel. The chic décor and somewhat adventurous menu make it a unique find in the Roswell suburb. Start with the crab cake or brick oven roasted oysters. Small plates of gnocchi and steak tartare are a steal at $12 or less. Fish and seafood entrees, with the exception of the short rib with spicy mac n cheese outshine meat entrees. $$$$

Breakers Korean 3505 Gwinnett Pl Dr. #101 Duluth, 30096; (770) 946-1000 www.breakersbbq.com

You don't have to make your way to Buford Highway to experience some of the best Korean barbecue. Breakers, located in Gwinnett, is an upscale spot, for newbies to Korean food. Korean barbecue restaurants have grills at tables where food is cooked in front of you. The only problem? You leave smelling like your food. Breakers generously installed ventilation systems that avoid all of this. Servers are used to patrons not well-versed in Korean foods and are willing to patiently explain the process. All of the meats – beef, pork belly, chicken, are scrumptious. *Must order:* **Bulgogi, a grilled marinated beef. $$**

Century House Tavern 125 E Main St, Woodstock, GA 30188; (770) 693-4552 www.centuryhousetavern.com

Located in historic downtown Woodstock, Century House Tavern is located in what was once The Hubbard House, named after the family that lived there for six decades. The house has been renovated nicely to serve as a restaurant, allowing for comfortable space without feeling overcrowded. Perfectly seared scallops, served over artichokes, English peas and fava beans are a delectable meal as is a Sous Vide tenderloin. An outstanding curated wine list should be taken advantage of. $$$

Colletta 900 3rd St, Alpharetta, GA 30009; (678) 722-8335
www.collettarestaurant.com

All pasta is not created the same as is evidenced by this
standout Avalon restaurant. Tip: You can play corn hole
outside the restaurant before or after dinner. Menu is
divided into Starters, Pizza, Pasta and Piatti (Entrees). Start
with the Arancini. Pizza is good, but the Pasta is better. A
simple Pappardelle with pork, tomato and ricotta impresses
as does the Agnolotti stuffed with short ribs and salsa verde.
$$$

Douceur de France 367 Glover St. Marietta, GA 30060;
(770) 425-5050 www.douceurdefrance.com

Word is that the owners believe making everything fresh
and from scratch, and the baking starts early each day. There
are usually a handful of French Nationals in the restaurants
at any given time, which attests to the authenticity of the
goods. The Quiche Lorraine is delicious. Although they have
various breakfast items and sandwiches, it is the desserts
and pastries that are the highlights at this authentic French
bakery. Don't miss the Almond Croissants or Macaroons.
Tip: If you like to bake, buy your butter here and you won't
regret it. Restaurant is closed on Sundays. $$

Drift Oyster and Fish House The Avenue East Cobb,
4475 Roswell Rd, Marietta, GA 30062; (770) 635-7641
www.driftoysterbar.com

East Cobb has been waiting quite some time for a seafood
spot to call their own, and it's finally arrived in Drift. From
the same owner as Seed Kitchen down the street, the beautiful appointed restaurant beckons you to forget you in a strip
mall. Indulge in low gravity cocktails at lunch. The Octopus

with a black pepper sauce is dazzling. Seafood like crab cakes, oysters and trout are so fresh, you'll think you are at a seaside restaurant instead of landlocked Atlanta. At dinner, the Halibut with smoked tomato butter is superb. $$$$

E.M. Bop 800 N Main St #130, Alpharetta, GA 30004; (678) 395-6226 www.embop.com

Chef and owner Yoon Choi cut his teeth at some of the most prestigious hotels in the country: The Four Seasons Chicago and the Beverly Hills Hotel, before opening EM Bop. Unlike most traditional Korean restaurants, there are no grills at table and no MSG is used. Start off with a Sochu cocktail and an order of their KFC, that's Korean Fried Chicken wings. Traditional Korean dishes like Bibimbap and Korean barbecue are tasty but so are Korean fusion dishes, like the chicken Bulgogi pasta. **$$**

Foundation Social Eatery 1570 Holcomb Bridge Rd Roswell, GA 30076; (770) 641-8877 www.foundationatl.com

The modern decor – light bright walls and dark wood floors mixed with rebar, yes, rebar, made me feel like I was at a swanky Midtown hot spot. Get the beet salad with strawberries and the fried Octopus to start. A Mushroom Ravioli dish is equally tasty. Besides a lot of garlic, there's the red wine truffle sauce and foamy texture. Earl Grey Chocolate Mousse takes the cake at Foundation Social Eatery! $$$

Henry's Louisiana Grill 4835 N Main St, Acworth, GA 30101; (770) 966-1515 www.chefhenrys.com

When dining at this fun Acworth restaurant, you really only need know three words...er....syllables: *Oh la la*. That's the name of the dish you must order. Fried shrimp, oysters or crawfish is tossed in a garlic cream sauce with Tasso and spinach and pasta. It is totally worth driving this far OTP for. Of course there's Etouffee, Jambalaya and other southern favorites. It gets crowded any given night so reservations are recommended. Closed on Sundays. $$

Kiosco – A Taste of Colombia 48 Powder Springs Rd., Marietta, GA 30060; (678) 337-7999 www.kioscocolombi-anrestaurant.com

This small restaurant (only about seven small tables are on the inside), is located along the outskirts of the Marietta Square, a popular destination for families, especially with the live bands and festivals on the weekends. The restaurant two most popular menu items are Empanadas and Tamales. The crispy Empanadas are filled with tender and tasty beef or chicken and their huge tamales come wrapped in a corn husk. The tender pork inside mixes well with the spicy habanero sauce poured atop it. The Carne con Pantacones, a shredded beef entrée with plantains is a dish full of flavor. At lunch, dishes come with choice of soup or bean salad. Lunch is served Monday through Saturday from 11 – 3pm. But it gets quite crowded. $$

Kurt's Bistro 3305 Peachtree Industrial Blvd #100, Duluth, GA 30096; (770) 623-4128 www.kurtsrestaurant.com

Named after its owner, Kurt Eisele, who has been running the restaurant for over 25 years, the restaurant is dimly lit perfect for a romantic date or a gathering of friends. European foods like Swiss Fondue, Escargot, and German sausages are found on the appetizer menu. The meat and cheese plate is a smart way to get a sampling of the authentically European meats and cheeses. Of course, the Wienerschnitzel or Jaegerschnitzel (breaded pork) are highlights. For a bit of everything, get the Schwabian Platter: smoked pork chop, bratwurst and Riesling braised sauerkraut. They also have a unique selection of brews, many which won't be found elsewhere. $$$

Made Kitchen and Cocktails 45 Roswell St Alpharetta, GA 30009; (770) 452-6233 www.madekc.com

Constructed from reclaimed wood from a South Carolina barn, MADE Kitchen and cocktails is a beautiful space with gorgeous features. There's a smallish bar located next to the open kitchen, if you want to pop in for craft cocktail, and maybe stay for some tapas. Get the Kentucky Creeper with bourbon, lavender honey and soda. There's also house made sangria (red or white), lots of draft beer and a well curated wine list, with nearly 30 different wines by the glass. Start with the grilled artichokes (this alone is worth the drive), with a touch of cream and paprika. Skip seafood dishes in favor of more substantial items like Braised Pork Cheeks topped with parsnip chips. Tip: It's a great place to dine before a concert at Verizon Wireless Amphitheatre. $$$

Madras Chettinaad 4305 State Bridge Road, Alpharetta, GA 30022; (678) 393-3131 www.madraschettinaad.com

This beautifully appointed Indian restaurant is outfitted with high-end furnishings, and relics from India. Once inside, it is easy to forget the strip mall locale. During weekdays, nearby office workers pack the restaurant at lunch time to take full advantage of the numerous buffet offerings. While there are plenty of vegetarian curries and dishes on the buffet, there are still a number of meat-centric entrees as well. The Chicken Tikka Masala and Chicken 65 are both highlights. At dinner, it's a more upscale affair. Start with Samosas. Thalis are a good option for those wishing to try a variety of small dishes, and Biryani rice dishes are tasty. However, curry dishes (lamb, chicken or shrimp) as well as the Butter Chicken are some of the best. Wash your meal down with a sweet Mango Lassi or refreshing coconut water. $$

Marietta Diner 306 Cobb Parkway, Marietta, GA 30060; (770) 423-9390 www.mariettadiner.net

The glowing neon signage illuminates the otherwise sleepy stretch of road during late hours. Upon entering the restaurant, patrons are immediately teased with the enormous display case of the decadent desserts that the diner has available. The diner serves breakfast, lunch and dinner each day and as such the menu (pages and pages long) has something for everyone. Patrons are treated to a complimentary spinach pie with each order. The portions are huge and most diners walk away with take out boxes, unable to finish a meal in one sitting. Service is always fast, friendly and efficient. Even if you are too stuffed to order dessert, choose one and take it with you to go. The German Chocolate cake and cheesecakes are quite extraordinary. The diner is open 24 hours a day, 7 days a week, and even on Holidays. In fact, it is even full on Thanksgiving and Christmas. $$

Mountain Biscuits 1718 Old Hwy 41 Marietta, GA 30060; (770) 419-3311

Located near the National Historic Site, Kennesaw Mountain National Battlefield, Mountain Biscuits is a popular stop for families on their way to or from visiting the mountain. The establishment itself is a rather small space but with its bright, yellow color it has a charming, country appeal. The small gravel parking lot fills up can get quite busy on weekend mornings when patrons flock there for a hearty breakfast biscuit. The biscuits here are huge. The meat inside biscuits is quality and the flavor comes through. Highlights are the bacon, egg and cheese, sausage and the chicken biscuits. The restaurant is open for lunch as well. Breakfast is served all day and lunch is served from 11 am to 2pm. Only open from 6 am until 2 pm. Closed on Sundays. $

Noble Fin 5260 Peachtree Parkway, Peachtree Corners, GA 30092; (770) 599-7979 www.noblefinrestaurant.com

When chef Jay Swift closed his popular spot, 4th & Swift, fans were stunned. He emerged with Noble Fin shorty after, albeit a bit of a drive from the trendy in-town spot where he began. Sit at the bar and enjoy happy hours featuring oysters or shrimp on select days of the week. A Broiled Octopus comes with patatas bravas and catija cheese. Beef Tartar is artfully presented with watercress mayo. Trout and Scallops served with polenta and pork belly are highlights. $$$

Oak Steakhouse 950 3rd St, Alpharetta, GA 30009; (678) 722-8333 www.oaksteakhouseatlanta.com

With a plethora of terrific steak options inside the perimeter, why venture to the burbs? Dry aged steak from Mastery Purveyors of NYC is why. The dry age process involved letting meat hang out in a cooler for about 21 days or more while allowing the flavors to develop fully. Though the dark woods and comfy leather booths have the feel of a traditional steakhouse, there's a modern energy the flows through the restaurant. And there are definite departures from the hackneyed menu items of typical steakhouse. Killer cocktails and mocktails are available. Other than steak, the Scallops and Pork Belly are outstanding as is the Agnolotti. Tip: Oak Steakhouse has an outstanding bar menu of items priced under $15. $$$$

O4W (Old Fourth Ward) Pizza 3117 Main Street, Duluth, GA 30096; (678) 587-5420 www.o4wpizza.com

Quickly amassing a cult-like following for their Jersey-style pizza, the small spot quickly outgrew its Irwin Street Market surroundings. Lucky for Duluth residents, they've taken up residence there. A simple cheese slice is magnificent. But the crowd favorite is the Grandpa Pie. It is thick Sicilian slices with basil, mozzarella, pecorino and sweet, robust marinara sauce. It's only available in one size, 16" you can upgrade to Veggie or Meatball toppings too. $

Osteria Mattone 1095 Canton St, Roswell, GA 30075; (678) 878-3378 www.osteriamattone.com

This remodeled house is has an open plan that still retains much of the charm it had as a dwelling. At lunch the Build Your Own Pizza is a terrific deal. However, it's certainly romantic as a weekend date option. Snuggle up to your sweetie outside near the fire pit on a cool fall evening while sipping on a glass of Chianti if you have to wait for a table. Appetizers like the Pulpo (Octopus) with mint are tasty and a Short Rib Agnolotti is magnificent too. Closed on Mondays. $$$

Specialty Market – Patak Meats, 4107 Ewing Road, Austell, GA 30106; (770) 941-7993 www.patakmeats.com

Steak, pork chops and sausages are what keep the patrons lined up to get here. Sausages of all varieties can be found here – it's literally a sausage fest. You can easily walk out with two or three bags of high-quality meat for under $40. Say goodbye to prepackaged, filler and nitrate-heavy meats. There is also a variety of Eastern European dry goods. Patrons drive long distances to shop here. The primarily Eastern

European staff is friendly, helpful and efficient. Closed on weekends. $$

Porch Light Latin Kitchen 300 Village Green Cir SE #110, Smyrna, GA 30080;

(678) 309-9858 www.porchlightlatinkitchen.com

Offering new twists on Latin dishes, is the vibrant restaurant breathing new life into Smyrna. Plantain Empanadas have shells made of plantains vs. dough and the Smashed Mofongo are made with yucca and served with a duck confit. Entrees like Mahi Tacos and a Beer Can Chicken Burrito are ridiculously good at lunch or dinner. Mixed with cilantro and rice, this chicken is so much more than shredded chicken from most burritos. And the house made sauces are a verdant addition to the meals. $$

Ray's Killer Creek 1700 Mansell Rd Alpharetta, GA 30009; (770) 649-0064 www.raysrestaurants.com

The high end steakhouse has always been a popular destination for business dinners, but also has more eclectic and lower priced options. Pricey, huge cuts of steaks like the gigantic ribeye are available, but other more affordable offerings to the menu like a flatbread of the day are executed well. The Veal Bolognese and Short Rib are other options that are high on taste, but a little lighter on the wallet. Reservations required. $$$$

The Rotisserie Shop 2615 George Busbee Pkwy, Kennesaw, GA 30144; (678) 540-8244 www.therotisserieshop.com

The cozy atmosphere is good for small groups or couples looking for a quick meal. Rotisserie is so juicy, you'll even see staff taking the chicken off of the large skewers, similar to what you find at the Brazilian steakhouses. You'll have your choice of dipping house made dipping sauces for your chicken. Some include Cilantro Lime Tomatillo or Wild Mushroom Marsala. Besides rotisserie, pulled pork and the like, they also offer catering that features Italian favorites like lasagna, eggplant parmigiana, baked ziti and more. They also offer picnic meals for 3-4 for around $20. Tip: They have $2 tacos on Tuesdays, plus other weekly specials. Save room for the Lemon Mascarpone Torta. $$

Salt Factory 952 Canton St Roswell, GA 30075; (770) 998-4850 www.saltfactorypub.com

Don't be fooled by the name, Salt Factory serves up some extremely tasty entrees in this rustic and historic building. The wood floor and exposed brick walls lend a rich yet cozy feel for this high-end pub. Located in the heart of Roswell, some patrons enjoy stopping for a pint, but it is the food that brought the Food Network here to profile the restaurant. The cheeses and charcuterie plate should not be missed. They even come with house made dipping sauces. The Shepherd's Pie however, is the dish that made it world famous, made with lamb instead of beef and spiked with cumin. Served in a cash iron skillet, it is definitely comfort food and a pretty large portion. Surprisingly, the wine list seems more robust than the beer list even though it is a pub. $$$

Swallow at the Hollow 1072 Green St Roswell, GA 30075; (678) 352-1975 www.theswallowatthehollow.com

Menu items here are prepared using organic and locally grown ingredients if possible. The ribs or chopped pork are solid and the sauce is quite tasty. Vegetarian options include Smoked Portabella Mushroom and Fried Green Tomatoes.

Regulars rave about the Mac 'n Cheese. Banana pudding has a unique twist, using chocolate chips instead of Nilla wafers. The porch and entire outdoor seating area is lovely. Tip: They have live music on weekends. Reservations aren't accepted so expect long wait times on weekends. $$

Table & Main 1028 Canton St, Roswell, GA 30075; (678) 869-5178 www.tableandmain.com

Located on the busy Canton street, this sister restaurant to Osteria Mattone is serving upscale Southern in a renovated home as well. Collard Greens, Fried Green Tomatoes and Hoppin' John can all be found on the menu. A beet salad is given a unique twist with beet puree and a 6 minute egg. For mains, pork is a good option, one with "Cheer Wine BBQ" and another with "Coca-Cola Balsamic", as are the Catfish and Trout. Tip: They keep a certain number of tables available for walk-ins and surprisingly the system works quite well. Closed on Mondays. $$$

Vin 25 25 Plum Tree St, Roswell, GA 30075; (770) 628-0411 www.vin25.com

Tucked away on a quiet neighborhood street in Roswell, Vin 25 seems like a secret oasis Roswellites keep to themselves. The cozy spot has a beautiful display of wines and dark wood inside, but when the weather is right, patio seating is prime. As the name suggests, Vin 25 is a wine bar. Their selection of wines by the glass is quite impressive, and serves are knowledgeable if you can't decide. The small menu, executed well, features items like lamb meatballs and lump crab flatbread. $$

Vingenzo's Woodstock, GA 105 E Main Street Suite 100, Woodstock, GA 30188; (770) 924-9133 www.vingenzos.com

Some of the best pasta and Neapolitan pizza can be found in this unassuming downtown Woodstock restaurant. Almost all ingredients are imported from Italy. There's a pasta machine, which cranks out three house made pastas each day. Even the mozzarella is made in house. Start the meal with the grandioso tasting, which comes with three different styles of mozzarella, and your choice of charcuterie. The quality ingredients used are evident in the pizza as well. Margerita, although simplistic was bursting with flavor as was the spicy Soppressata and Taggiasche olives. Try at least one pizza when visiting. As for pastas, the house specialty is the Sugo Di Domenica'. This is a rich tomato sauce complimented by tasty shreds of pork. Wine selection is carefully curated, yet very affordable. $$$

CHAPTER 10
Local Chains

Every city has a couple restaurants that are chain restaurants only within their city border. These are restaurants that locals love no matter what their preference of food is. These restaurants are pleasing to all Atlantans. They've been around for quite a while and garnered a loyal following.

Café Intermezzo www.cafeintermezzo.com

Although Café Intermezzo has a food menu, it is the desserts and coffees that have been dazzling patrons for years. The interior is a beautiful space in and of itself with cozy tables and candlelight. The coffee / drink menu, it is thicker than the food menu. Full of exotic kinds of coffees, teas, drinks, etc. If a nutty taste is what you like with a hint of sweetness, opt for the Suisse Mokka or the Spanish Mokka, two of my favorites. For non-coffee drinkers give the Mexican Chocolate a try, a dessert by itself for sure. True coffee connoisseurs will appreciate the Turkish coffee, which comes in its own carafe. The desserts change daily. Once seated, make your way to the dessert display case and choose from their many cheesecakes and pies. The attendant will write your selection down and give it to you, which you hand to your server once back at your table. A little unorthodox, but all part of their kitsch. $

El Taco Veloz www.tacoveloz.com

With a handful of Atlanta locations, this authentic taco joint is barely a chain. The smallish tacos pack a lot of flavor in them. Two corn soft taco shells envelope the meat and other goodies inside each taco to help keep the filling inside. Two to three will fill you up. The El Pastor (Pork) is one of the best on the menu although the Barbacoa (Brisket) is quite tasty as well. Don't expect chips and salsa with your meal. Staff doesn't speak much English, but it is relatively easy to decipher the menu. Tacos are around two dollars. They also have tasty tortas, burritos and tamales. Don't miss out on having a Horchata with your meal. This is a sweet drink made with rice milk. $

Fellinis Pizza www.fellinisatlanta.com

All locations of this late night pizza favorite are located inside the Perimeter. While all seven locations are open until midnight, several are open until 2 am. Visitors come here not only for the fantastic pizza, but also the lively atmosphere and vibrant decor. Many Fellini's pizzas are located in former garages that have been refurbished, incorporating old elements like doors to the new design. Many also feature large outdoor patios that patrons fill up on warm days and evenings. As for the pizza, it can be ordered by the pie or by the slice. By the slice is far more popular. Pepperoni and sausage are certainly winners as is the Spinach and mushroom. Slices are huge and one slice should satisfy a normal appetite. Salad here is also very large and comes with quality ingredients including lots of fresh mozzarella and black olives. Groups love to order pitchers of beers and leisurely enjoy their pizza. $

Flying Biscuit www.flyingbiscuit.com

Open for breakfast, lunch and dinner, stop in anytime but don't miss out on the biscuits. Flying Biscuit makes 5,000 per week per location. Another reason to love Flying Biscuit? They serve breakfast all day every day. Their Clifton Omelet stuffed with goat cheese and mushroom is outstanding but so is a Coca-Cola Chicken Burrito. The bright and busy atmosphere is perfect for families.

La Fonda Latina www.fellinisatlanta.com/lafonda.html

Sister restaurant to Fellini's Pizza, the two are *usually* located next door to one another. This is a highlight as far as inexpensive Latin Food. The food is delivered quickly in a fun atmosphere (opt for outdoor seating whenever possible). The ingredients are always fresh and high quality. Don't miss out on the Beef Enchiladas, Spinach and Shrimp Quesadillas, Vegetarian Paella or Arroz con Pollo (chicken and rice). $

Marlow's www.marlowstavern.com

Each Marlow's location is built with the same design and layout. Marlow's is not your ordinary Pub. The upscale establishment features better than your average pub fare in a friendly atmosphere. What's incredible is that Marlow's has managed to expand their footprint across the Atlanta area over the last several years, but has been able to do so without losing their uniqueness. The Firecracker shrimp is a must for me each visit, with crispy, spicy shrimp. Tuna Poke is quite a generous portion and their burgers are wonderful. $$

Meehan's www.meehanspublichouse.com

Another pub style restaurant that has expanded rapidly is Meehan's Irish Pub. Meehan's may be a pub, but their food is anything but pub-like. For starters, Ahi tuna bites are chopped tuna atop an English cucumber with pickled ginger and feta. And how do you put an interesting twist on hummus? Use a mixture of Edamame and goat cheese for a delicious and unique dip. If you are eating light, there are plenty of salads to choose from as well. Grilled cheese is made with Feta. They also have delicious entrees, many of which are gluten free.

CHAPTER 11
Not Starbucks

Adios Café (Castleberry Hill) 180 Walker St., Atlanta, GA 30312; (404) 574-5678 www.adioscafe.com

Stop in for coffee between 8 am and 10 pm. A specialty is Café de Olla, Traditional Mexican coffee with a hint of cinnamon and cocoa. They also serve breakfast and specialties include The Adios - Chorizo hash browns topped with 2 eggs or Mexican Eggs Benedict - 2 poached eggs, bacon and green chile hollandaise, atop a house made masa cake.

Chattahoochee Coffee Company 6640 Akers Mill Rd Atlanta, GA 30339; (770) 955-0788 www.chattahoocheecoffee.com

Though it can be a challenge to locate this coffee shop, located inside a gated apartment community, the payoff is worth it, with the location along the banks of the Chattahoochee. When the secret got out about its breathtaking views and serene environment, rules changed to only let non-residents in Monday through Fridays. But the French Press is worth it. You are limited to two hours of parking.

Condesa 480 John Wesley Dobbs Ave Ste 100 Atlanta, GA 30312; (404) 524-5054 www.condesacoffee.com

The coffee is good, but the lattes are better, especially the chai tea lattes. There's also craft beer, wine and cocktails available. Parking can be a bit difficult. Walk if at all possible. Get the pretzel croissants too.

Copper Coin 705 Town Blvd Ste 510 Atlanta, GA 30319; (404) 600-8340 www.coppercoincoffee.com

This modern designed coffee house has terrific coffee and is a great option for a business meeting. If you get hungry the spicy egg sandwich will fill you up. They are even open at dinner and serve beer and wine. Caveats: Parking can be sparse and after two hours, you must purchase a new item to keep using Wi-Fi.

Corso Coffee The Shops Buckhead Atlanta, 3065 Peachtree Rd NE #210, Atlanta, GA 30305; (678) 553-9009 www.corsocoffee.com/atlanta

Located at the Shops at Buckhead Atlanta is the sleek and posh Corso. Sure, there's Espresso and Macchiato here. But you can also find reasonably priced breakfast and lunch items. A Savory Croissant with Eggs and Fontina is quite reasonable. Plus there are daily specials like a Shrimp Roll and Chicken and Waffles. Plus wine is available in the evenings. They offer afternoon tea Thursdays, Fridays and Saturdays from 3-5 pm. This includes a selection of teas, sandwiches, French Macarons and other pastries.

Dancing Goats 650 North Ave, Atlanta, GA 30308; www.batdorfcoffee.com/retail-locations.html/#atlanta

Many high end Atlanta restaurants procure their coffee from Batdorf and Bronson, a small roaster with locations in both Atlanta and Olympia Washington. They also operate the Dancing Goats Coffee. You can find them at the trendy Ponce City Market. There's a fantastic patio – grab a swing if you find a free one.

Dr. Bombay's Underwater Tea Party 1645 McLendon Ave, Atlanta, GA 30307; (404) 474-1402 www.drbombays.com

It's got a funny name but this coffee and tea shop serves a good purpose. They help impoverished girls in India with the profits made here. The walls are lined with books, so feel free to peruse if you need a break from work. They also take reservations for tea parties.

Inman Perk 240 N Highland Ave Atlanta, GA 30307; (678) 705-4545 www.inmanperkcoffee.com

This family owned coffee shop has been open for longer than most coffee shops in Atlanta. Get an Iced Dirty Chai, tea and espresso. Staff often seems indifferent but it is a quiet place to work or study if you need it. They have sandwiches, ice cream and there fruit smoothies are pretty tasty.

JavaVino 579 N Highland Ave Atlanta, GA 30307; (404) 577-8673 www.javavino.com

Need a little pick me up or booze me up? Either way, you're covered at JavaVino. As the name suggests, the coffee shop serves both coffee and wine. Get the Caramel Breve. You can also grab dinner here as well and if you don't eat meat, you're in luck, as there are lots of vegetarian items.

Land of A Thousand Hills (Atlantic Station) 232 19th St #7100 Atlanta, GA 30363; (470) 344-0197 www.lando-fathousandhills.com/atlanticstation

They offer Rwandan coffee that supports the local farmers in the country. The original location of is in the suburbs of Roswell, but the Midtown location is quite nice too. Look for seasonal specialties like Pumpkin Pie or Apple Cider. An Iced Caramanilla in the summer is perfect. Plus, there's plenty of outdoor seating too. Tip: Park in the purple section near stairwell 3 for easy access to the coffee shop.

Octane 1009 Marietta St Atlanta, GA 30318; (404) 815-9886 www.octanecoffee.com

This trendy spot, located on the Westside is catnip for hipster freelancers. Inside you'll find concrete floors, exposed ductwork and brick walls. For a sufficient, yet tasty jolt get the Americans (double shot). There are sandwiches and other treats from local purveyors available too. There are now locations in Buckhead and Grant Park as well.

Paris Baguette 5252 Buford Hwy Doraville, GA 30340; (770) 455-8552 www.parisbaguetteusa.com

Hailing from South Korea, there are some locations in California and New York, but this is the only location in the Southeast. Besides coffee, you can find lovely Korean pastries and bubble tea here. If you are looking for cronuts, here's where you can find them. For the best selection of pastries, visit in the morning as by the afternoon, there's far less of a selection. Note: No Wi-Fi is available.

Revelator 691 14th St Atlanta, GA 30318; www.revelatorcoffee.com

This small chain originated in Birmingham, AL, but has a location on the Westside. Parking and Wi-Fi are both free here. Espresso has a distinct nutty flavor. Chemex pour-overs are the brew method of choice, and they rotate with seasonally sourced coffees. The modern, minimalist décor is the perfect to have a quiet meeting or catch up with a friend.

Spiller Park Ponce City Market 675 Ponce de Leon Avenue Atlanta, Ga. 30308; (404) 919-2978 www.spillerpark.com

With the snazzy Ponce City Market location, located in the middle of the food hall, they've got a captive audience and you'll certainly pay for the location. Tip: You can get a Sublime Doughnut (some of the best in the city) here too.

Warhorse Coffee (Goat Farm) 1200 Foster St Atlanta, GA 30318; (407) 731-1557

Located on property with a former Cotton Gin Factory, its claim to fame is that an episode of The Walking Dead was filmed here. The decor consists of nostalgic items like typewriters, rotary phones, and vintage furniture. Coffee is free, but donations are accepted so make sure to bring cash. It can be tricky to find, park in the gravel lot and head toward the buildings following the path on the right down the stairs and you'll find the coffee house.

CHAPTER 12
Breweries

Georgia is a fantastic state to call home, except for a couple things – one of them being ridiculous blue laws. Why Georgia is still just one of a handful of states where brewers are not allowed to sell their beer directly to consumers baffles me. The good news is, that hasn't stopped many breweries from opening up all around Atlanta. To get around these pesky blue laws, breweries let patrons buy a "glass" which comes with tasting tickets you can have before or after you tour the facility. Here are the breweries you will want to make sure you visit. Note that open hours, specials, and brews do change. So make sure to verify this before visiting each brewery.

Jekyll Brewing 2855 Marconi Dr Ste 350. Alpharetta, GA 30005; (844) 453-5955 www.jekyllbrewing.com

Live on the north side? Head on over to Jekyll Brewing in Alpharetta. They have a fun space and plenty of games to play while sipping on the 'Merican Amber with caramel notes and spicy finish. Tip: Visit on Tuesdays for a special release that won't ever be made again. Taproom is open Tuesday through Saturday.

Monday Night Brewing 670 Trabert Ave Atlanta, GA 30318; (404) 352-7703 www.mondaynightbrewing.com

With a slogan that "Weekends are Overrated" they hold true to that with brewery tours on Mondays, Tuesdays and Thursdays from 5:30 – 7:30. They do make an exception on Saturdays with tours from 1-4. If you like wheat, don't miss the Fu Manbrew. IPA lovers shouldn't miss the Eye Patch Ale. Luckily you aren't far from the West Midtown hot restaurants after your tour is over.

Orpheus 1440 Dutch Valley Pl Atlanta, GA 30324; (404) 347-1777 www.orpheusbrewing.com

You couldn't ask for a better location: overlooking Piedmont Park and the Atlanta Beltline. They have a terrific selection of IPAs and Sours. Probably their most talked about beer is the Plum Saison. Bring your dog as they are dog friendly. Tip: They also have a comedy night the first Wednesday of every month from 7:30-10:30 p.m. Tours are Thursday through Sundays.

Red Brick Brewing 2323 Defoor Hills Rd Atlanta, GA 30318; (404) 881-0300 www.redbrickbrewing.com

The oldest craft brewer in the state, Red Brick has been at it for greater than 20 years. The brewery is also located in West Midtown, so you can visit one of the trendy restaurants after the tour. The brewery is open to the public Wednesday – Friday from 5-8pm and on Saturday (11 am – 5 pm), Sunday 1-4 pm. One highlight is that they allow patrons to bring in food from nearby establishments. So, feel free to pick something up on the way and enjoy it while sipping on some of their beer. During warm months, the crew even sets up fun games outside like Ping Pong and Corn Hole. Tip: Visit on Wednesdays to try a new brew that is not available anywhere else. Friday evenings feature live music.

Reformation Brewery 500 Arnold Mill Way Ste A Woodstock, GA 30188; (678) 341-0828 www.reformationbrewery.com

Located north of Atlanta, in Woodstock, you wouldn't expect such delicious brews hidden away in what appears to be an office complex. But it's worth seeking out, as they let their beers sit on yeast for a full three weeks as opposed to just one week of other beers, rendering better flavor. All the beers (yes, I've pretty much tried them all!) are outstanding. Get the Stark Porter if available. It is made with toasted coconut. Tours are every Thursday, Friday and Saturday.

Scofflaw Brewing 1738 MacArthur Blvd, Atlanta, GA 30318

Scofflaw is the newest brewery in Atlanta. The brewery offers four different kinds of beers, including two versions of an IPA- their Basement IPA and the Westside IPA. They also have a Pale Ale (Slim the Pale Ale) and a Wheat Beer (Sneaky Wheat). The Westside IPA is particularly refreshing, with a crispness and note of caramel. The fourth offering in the lineup is Sneaky Wheat. Aptly named, with its high ABV of 8 percent it can sneak up on you.

Second Self Beer Company 1317 Logan Cir, Atlanta, GA 30318; (678) 916-8035   www.secondselfbeer.com

Thai Wheat is one of the most popular beers, brewed with lemongrass and ginger. A Red Hop Rye IPA is designed to pair with spicy foods. But the most unique beer has to be the Mole Porter, brewed with chocolate and chilies. Tours are $12, and, though tour days vary, Fridays at 6 p.m. seem to be a consistent time.

Sweetwater Brewery 195 Ottley Dr. Atlanta, GA 30324 (404) 691-2537   www.sweetwaterbrew.com

Sweetwater Brewery tours are every Wednesday, Thursday, and Friday evenings and Saturdays from 2:30 to 4:30. During weekdays, the doors to Sweetwater Brewery open at 5:30 and they have about 3 tours per evening every half an hour beginning at 6. Also, plan on eating before or after as there are no munchies offered. Parking fills up quickly, but is available throughout the various lots near the Brewery. The neighboring businesses are closed by then and allow patrons to park in the lots for free. They also have a great space for private events.

Three Taverns Brewery 121 New St Decatur, GA 30030; (404) 600-3355 www.threetavernsbrewery.com

Three Taverns' Decatur space is cozy and comfortable with lots of brick and wood ceilings. Unique to them is their take on Belgian style. Tip: Ride your bike to the tasting room and get $2 off your tour. Plus tours are free on your birthday. Tours are Thursdays, Fridays, Saturdays and some Sundays. Note: They will NOT let you idle inside even a minute before they open, (no matter what the weather is like) until their posted open times!

Wild Heaven Brewery 135b Maple St Decatur, GA 30030; (404) 997-8589 www.wildheavencraftbeers.com

Located in Decatur, you can visit one of the lovely Decatur restaurants after you visit the Wild Heaven Brewery. Their beer lineup includes Belgian style Golden Ale (Invocation) as well as Saison (White Blackbird). Looking for something that is more mellow and light? Try the Emergency Drinking Beer Pilsner Session Ale. Open 5:30 – 8:30 Thursdays and Fridays and Saturdays 2-6pm. All ages welcome on Sunday afternoons 2-5pm.

Urban Tree Cidery 1465 Howell Mill Road, Atlanta GA 30318; (404) 855-5446 www.urbantreecider.com

Urban Tree Cidery is truly a family business with the entire Resuta family involved in the business. Did you know? Cideries don't have to follow the same utterly ridiculous rules that apply to breweries when it comes to tasting? That means no silly "tasting tickets" to buy. Belly up to the bar and order whatever cider you'd like to try. Plus, they also serve craft beer and cocktails. And everything you'll find behind the bar is Georgia made! Different kinds of ciders are semi-sweet, semi-dry, and even barrel ages. Some ciders (like the Original semi-dry cider) taste more like a crisp white wine and some, like the Fugg'n Hopped, taste much like a beer. So, if you have a group of wine and beer lovers, this is a good middle ground. Buy a draft of any cider (priced between $5 and $7). Or get a growler – $23 including the bottle or $18 for refills.

CHAPTER 13
Food Tours & Top Chefs

Downtown Food Walks www.atlantafoodwalks.com

Lead by a lawyer turned tour operator, Akila McConnell, the Atlanta Food Walks are just as much full of historical insights as much as belly filling southern food. This Atlanta Food Walks tour is a terrific choice for those that are visiting Atlanta as well as those that don't venture to downtown often. Even if you've lived in Atlanta for a while there is still quite a bit you'll glean about the Castleberry Hill downtown neighborhood featured on this food tour. You'll visit a restaurant that played an important role in the Civil Rights Movement and you'll also visit Atlanta's oldest market, rich in culinary history. If you contact them in advance they can accommodate most food restrictions.

Tour Info:

When: Thursdays, Fridays, and Saturdays at 11 a.m.

Duration: Around 3.5 hours

Cost: $65 adults, $45 children (ages 12 and younger)

What's included: 15 food and drink tastings at 7 restaurants

Marietta Food Tours www. mariettafoodtours.com

In the northern suburbs of Atlanta, is the adorable Marietta Square, but don't dismiss it as lacking culture. Go around the globe without leaving the square on Marietta Culinary Tours. Australian Bakery Café is just one of the fantastic stops. With lots of supplies that would make any Aussie expat feel at home (Can you say Vegemite sandwich?), the hopping restaurant serves a plethora of meat pies, but that's not what you'll sample. It's a special off menu item. The tour would be an incredible afternoon if you've got out of town guests and are looking for something unique to entertain them. Plus, there's still plenty of wandering around, window shopping or if you are like me, Bubble Tea drinking, after the tour ends. Tip: Your guide book includes coupons and at least a couple make it worth holding on to.

Tour Info:

When: Saturdays @ 11 am

Duration: 3 hours

Cost: $45 (Buy 3 get one free)

What's included: Food Tour with 7 Tastes

Peachtree Food Tours www.peachtreefoodtours.com

Much like Atlanta Food Walks, there's a great deal of history involved. You'll hear about the transformation of the famed Peachtree Street over the decades. Owner/operator John Hannula, an Atlanta resident for nearly two decades, shares his knowledge of the city's architectural history, and his gregarious nature makes him a wonderful tour leader. As a former home builder, he is articulate in describing the gorgeous buildings along Peachtree Street. This tour is a fantastic introduction for newcomers to the city or those of you just visiting. Not only does the tour make stops at unique spots that exemplify Southern food, but Hannula offers insider tips for other places you must visit. Unlike the other tours, some alcohol is included in this food tour. Tour size is limited to eight to make for an intimate experience.

Tour Info:

When: Fridays (10:30 am), Saturdays (10 am) and Sundays (Noon)

Duration: 4-5 hours

Cost: $100

What's included: 5 Stops

Top Chef Alumni

Throughout the seasons of the Popular Television show "Top Chef" Atlanta has had much representation in the form of our very talented chefs. Atlantans have been very supportive of our skilled chefs and have made sure that these chefs continue to thrive in the city by supporting their restaurants. Some of these chefs have gone on to open several restaurants in the Atlanta area and have enjoyed lots of success due to the support from patrons.

Richard Blais

Probably the most famous Atlanta Chef due to Top Chef, Richard Blais, came close being crowned Top Chef in Season 4, but ultimately came in second place. Blais is known for putting his own personal style on traditional culinary cuisine. In Atlanta, Blais opened the hotter than hot restaurant, FLIP

Burger. These gourmet burgers are served up in a fun and lively atmosphere. FLIP has two locations: one in Buckhead and the original, in the trendy West Midtown area. Fun facts about Blais: He thinks everyone should keep Duck Fat in their pantry. He also was inspired to become a Chef after working at McDonald's as a teen. He found the camaraderie in the kitchen to be very energetic and pleasing and knew he wanted to make that his career.

Tracey Bloom

Tracey Bloom had a brief on Top Chef in Season Eight. She has spent much time at top restaurants in Atlanta including 103 West in Buckhead, Sia's, and Table 1280 in Midtown. Chef Bloom now works as a private chef and is passionate about Gluten Free eating.

Kevin Gillespie

Since appearing on Top Chef, Kevin has gone on write several successful cookbooks. Plus, he has two restaurants in some of the trendiest neighborhoods in Atlanta. Revival is his take on Southern food and Communion is the backyard beer garden. Gunshow was quick to have guests clamoring for its non-traditional dim sum fare.

Hector Santiago

After a brief stint on Top Chef in Season Six, Chef Santiago didn't let that slow him down. His wildly popular restaurant, Pura Vida that served Latin tapas was the inspiration for his new restaurant, Super Pan. Located in Ponce City Market, the restaurant features Cuban sandwiches and other delicious Latin goodies.

Made in the USA
Columbia, SC
31 January 2022